I0128258

Dinah Maria Mulock Craik

Little Sunshine's Holiday

A Picture from Life

Dinah Maria Mulock Craik

Little Sunshine's Holiday
A Picture from Life

ISBN/EAN: 9783337294168

Printed in Europe, USA, Canada, Australia, Japan

Cover: Foto ©Thomas Meinert / pixelio.de

More available books at **www.hansebooks.com**

LITTLE SUNSHINE'S HOLIDAY:

A PICTURE FROM LIFE.

BY THE

AUTHOR OF "JOHN HALIFAX, GENTLEMAN."

LITTLE SUNSHINE'S FRIENDS.
(*From a Photograph.*)

NEW YORK:
HARPER & BROTHERS, PUBLISHERS,
FRANKLIN SQUARE.
1871.

BY THE AUTHOR OF "JOHN HALIFAX."

———o———

HANNAH. Illustrated. 8vo, Paper.

LITTLE SUNSHINE'S HOLIDAY. A Story for Girls. Illustrated. 16mo, Cloth, 90 cents.

FAIR FRANCE. Impressions of a Traveler. 12mo, Cloth, $1 50.

A BRAVE LADY. Illustrated. 8vo, Paper, $1 00; Cloth, $1 50.

THE UNKIND WORD, AND OTHER STORIES. 12mo, Cloth, $1 50.

THE WOMAN'S KINGDOM. A Love Story. Illustrated. 8vo, Paper, $1 00 · Cloth, $1 50.

THE TWO MARRIAGES. 12mo, Cloth, $1 50.

A NOBLE LIFE. 12mo, Cloth, $1 50.

CHRISTIAN'S MISTAKE. 12mo, Cloth, $1 50.

JOHN HALIFAX, GENTLEMAN. 8vo, Paper, 75 cents; Library Edition, 12mo, Cloth, $1 50.

A LIFE FOR A LIFE. 8vo, Paper, 50 cents; Library Edition, 12mo, Cloth, $1 50.

A HERO, AND OTHER TALES. 12mo, Cloth, $1 25.

AGATHA'S HUSBAND. 8vo, Paper, 50 cents; 12mo, Cloth, $1 50.

AVILLION, AND OTHER TALES. 8vo, Paper, $1 25.

OLIVE. 8vo, Paper, 50 cents; 12mo, Cloth, $1 50.

THE FAIRY BOOK. The best popular Fairy Stories selected and rendered anew. Illustrated. 12mo, Cloth, $1 50.

THE HEAD OF THE FAMILY. 8vo, Paper, 75 cents; 12mo, Cloth, $1 50.

MISTRESS AND MAID. A Household Story. 8vo, Paper, 50 cents.

NOTHING NEW. Tales. 8vo, Paper, 50 cents.

THE OGILVIES. Tales. 8vo, Paper, 50 cents; 12mo, Cloth, $1 50.

OUR YEAR. A Child's Book in Prose and Verse. Illustrated by Clarence Dobell. 16mo, Cloth, Gilt Edges, $1 00.

STUDIES FROM LIFE. 12mo, Cloth, Gilt Edges, $1 25.

A FRENCH COUNTRY FAMILY. Translated from the French of Madame De Witt (née Guizot). Illustrated. 12mo, Cloth, $1 50.

MOTHERLESS. A Story for Girls in their Teens. Translated from the French of Madame De Witt (née Guizot). Illustrated. 12mo, Cloth, 50.

———o———

Published by HARPER & BROTHERS, New York.

☞ Sent by mail, postage prepaid, to any part of the United States, on receipt of the price.

Dedicated

TO

LITTLE SUNSHINE'S LITTLE FRIENDS.

CONTENTS.

ILLUSTRATIONS.

LITTLE SUNSHINE'S
HOLIDAY.

CHAPTER I.

WHILE writing this title, I paused, considering whether the little girl to whom it refers would not say of it, as she sometimes does of other things, "You make a mistake." For she is such a very accurate little person. She can not bear the slightest alteration of a fact. In herself and in other people she must have the truth, the whole truth, and nothing but the truth. For instance, one day, overhearing her mamma say, "I had my shawl with me," she whispered, "No, mamma, not your shawl; it was your water-proof."

Therefore, I am sure she would wish me to explain at once that "Little Sunshine" is not her real name, but a pet name, given because she is such a sunshiny child; and that her "holiday" was not so much hers—seeing she

was then not three years old, and every day
was a holiday—as her papa's and mamma's,
who are very busy people, and who took her
with them on one of their rare absences from
home. They felt they could not do without her merry laugh, her little pattering feet,
and her pretty curls—even for a month. And
so she got a "holiday" too; though it was
quite unearned : as she has never been to
school, and her education has gone no farther
than a crooked *S*, a round *O*, an *M* for mamma, and a *D* for—but this is telling.

Of course Little Sunshine has a Christian
name and surname, like other little girls, but I
do not choose to give them. She has neither
brother nor sister, and says " she doesn't want
any—she had rather play with papa and mamma." She is not exactly a pretty child, but
she has very pretty yellow curls, and is rather
proud of " my curls." She has only lately begun to say " I " and " my," generally speaking
of herself, baby-fashion, in the third person—
as " Sunny likes that," " Sunny did so-and-so,"
etc. She always tells every thing she has done
and every thing she is going to do. If she
has come to any trouble—broken a tea-cup, for
instance—and her mamma says, " Oh, I am so
sorry ! Who did that ?" Little Sunshine will

creep up, hanging her head and blushing, "Sunny did it; she won't ever do it again." But the idea of denying it would never come into her little head. Every body has always. told the exact truth to her, and so she tells the truth to every body, and has no notion of there being such a thing as falsehood in the world.

Still, this little girl is not a perfect character. She sometimes flies into a passion, and says "I won't" in a very silly way—it is always so silly to be naughty. And sometimes she feels thoroughly naughty—as we all do occasionally—and then she says, of her own accord, "Mamma, Sunny had better go into the cupboard" (her mamma's dressing-closet). There she stays, with the door close shut, for a little while; and then comes out again smiling, "Sunny is quite good now." She kisses mamma, and is all right. This is the only punishment she has ever had—or needed, for she never sulks, or does any thing underhand or mean or mischievous; and her wildest storm of passion only lasts a few minutes. To see mamma looking sad and grave, or hear her say, "I am so sorry that my little girl is naughty," will make the child good again immediately.

So you have a faint idea of the little person who was to be taken on this long holiday; first

B

in a " puff-puff," then in a boat—which was to
her a most remarkable thing, as she lives in a
riverless county, and, except once crossing the
Thames, had scarcely ever beheld water. Her
mamma had told her, however, of all the wonderful things she was to see on her holiday;
and for a week or two past she had been saying to every visitor that came to the house,
" Sunny is going to Scotland. Sunny is going
in a puff-puff to Scotland. And papa will take
her in a boat, and she will catch a big salmon.
Would you like to see Sunny catch a big salmon?" For it is the little girl's firm conviction that to see Sunny doing any thing must be
the greatest possible pleasure to those about
her—as perhaps it is.

Well, the important day arrived. Her mamma was very busy, Little Sunshine helping her
—to " help mamma" being always her grand
idea. The amount of work she did, in carrying her mamma's clothes from the drawers to
the portmanteau, and carrying them back
again; watching her dresses being folded and
laid in the trunk, then jumping in after them,
smoothing and patting them down, and, lastly,
sitting upon them, can not be told. Every now
and then she looked up, " Mamma, isn't Sunny
a busy girl?"—which could not be denied.

The packing-up was such a great amusement—to herself, at least—that it was with difficulty she could be torn from it, even to get her dinner, and be dressed for her journey, part of which was to take place that day. At last she was got ready, a good while before any body else, and then she stood and looked at herself from head to foot in a large mirror, and was very much interested in the sight. Her travelling-dress was a gray water-proof cloak, with a hood and pockets, where she could carry all sorts of things—her gloves, a biscuit, the head of her dolly (its body had come off), and two or three pebbles, which she daily picked up in the garden, and kept to wash in her bath night and morning, " to make them clean," for she has an extraordinary delight in things being " quite clean." She had on a pair of new boots—buttoned boots, the first she ever had— and she was exceedingly proud of them, as well as of her gray felt hat, underneath which was the usual mass of curly yellow hair. She shook it from side to side like a little lion's mane, calling out, " Mamma, look at Sunny's curls! Such a lot of curls !"

When the carriage came to the door, she watched the luggage being put in very gravely. Then all the servants came to say good-bye to her. They were very kind servants, and very fond of Little Sunshine. Even the gardener and his wife looked quite sorry to part with her, but in her excitement and delight the little lady of course did not mind it at all.

"Good-bye! good-bye! I'm going to Scotland," she kept saying, and kissing her hand. "Sunny's going to Scotland in a puff-puff. But she'll come back again, she will."

After which kind promise, meant to cheer them up a little, she insisted on jumping into the carriage "all by her own self,"—she dearly likes doing any thing "all my own self"—and, kissing her hand once more, was driven away with her mamma and her nurse (whose name is Lizzie) to meet her papa in London.

Having been several times in a " puff-puff," and once in London, she was not a bit frightened at the streets or the crowd. Only in the confusion at Euston Square she held very tight to her mamma's hand, and at last whispered, "Mamma, take her! up in you arms, up in you own arms!"—her phrase when she was almost a baby. And though she is now a big girl, who can walk, and even run, she clung tightly to her mamma's neck, and would not be set down again until transferred to her papa, and taken by him to look at the engine.

Papa and his little girl are both very fond of engines. This was such a large one, newly painted, with its metal-work so clean and shiny, that it was quite a picture. Though sometimes it gave a snort, and a puff, like a live creature, Sunny was not afraid of it, but sat in her papa's arms watching it, and then walked gravely up and down with him, holding his hand, and making all sorts of remarks on the things she saw, which amused him exceedingly. She also informed him of what she was going to do—how she should jump into the puff-puff, and then jump out again, and sleep in a cottage, in a quite new bed, where Sunny had never slept before. She chattered so fast, and was so delighted at every thing about her, that the time went rapidly by; and her papa, who could not come to Scotland for a week yet, was obliged to leave her. When he kissed her, poor Little Sunshine set up a great cry.

"I don't want you to go away. Papa! papa!" Then bursting in to one of her pathetic little furies, "I won't let papa go away! I won't!"

She clung to him so desperately that her little arms had fairly to be untied from round his neck, and it was at least two minutes and a half before she could be comforted.

But when the train began to move, and the carriageful of people to settle down for the journey, Sunny recovered herself, and grew interested in watching them. They were all gentlemen, and as each came in, mamma had suggested that if he objected to a child, he had better choose another carriage; but nobody did. One—who looked like the father of a family— said: "Ma'am, he must be a very selfish kind of man who does object to children—that is, good children." So mamma earnestly hoped that hers would be a good child.

So she was—for a long time. There were such interesting things to see out of the window: puff-puffs without end: some moving on the rails—some standing still—some with a long train behind them—some without. What perplexed and troubled Little Sunshine most, was to see the men who kept running across the rails and ducking under the engines. She got quite excited about them.

"That poor man must not go on the rails, else the puff-puff will run over him and hurt him. Then Sunny must pick him up, and take him to her nursery, and cuddle him." (She always wants to cuddle every body who is ill or hûrt.) "Mamma, tell that poor man he *mustn't* go on the rails."

And even when mamma explained that the man knew what he was about, and was not likely to let himself be run over by any puff-puff, the little girl still looked anxious and unhappy, until the train swept right away into the open country, with fields and trees, and cows and baa-lambs. These last delighted her much. She kept nodding her head and counting them. "There's papa baa-lambs, and mamma baa-lambs, and little baby baa-lambs, just like Little Sunny; and they all run about together; and they are so happy."

Every thing, indeed, looked as happy as the lambs and the child. It was a bright September day, the trees just beginning to change color, and the rich midland counties of England—full of farms and pasture-lands, with low hills sloping up to the horizon—looked specially beautiful. But the people in the carriage did not seem to notice any thing. They were all gentlemen, as I said, and they had all got their afternoon papers, and were reading hard. Not much wonder, as the newspapers were terribly interesting that day—the day after the capitulation of Sedan, when the Emperor Louis Napoleon surrendered himself and his army to King William of Prussia. When Little Sunshine has grown a woman, she will understand

all about it. But now she only sat looking at
the baa-lambs out of the window, and now and
then pulling, rather crossly, at the newspaper
in her mamma's hand. " I don't want you to
read!" In her day, may there never be read
such dreadful things as her mamma read in
those newspapers!

The gentlemen at last put down theirs, and
began to talk together, loudly and fast. Sunshine's mamma listened, now to them, now to
her little girl, who asked all sorts of questions, .
as usual. " What's that? you tell me about
that," she is always saying, as she twists her
fingers tight in those of her mamma, who an-
swers at once, and exactly, so far as she knows.
When she does not know—and even mammas
can not be expected to understand every thing
—she says plainly, "My little girl, I don't
know." And her little girl always believes her,
and is satisfied.

Sunshine was growing rather tired now ; and
the gentlemen kept on talking, and did not
take any notice of her, or attempt to amuse her,
as strangers generally do, she being such a lively and easily-amused child. Her mamma, fear-
ful of her restlessness, struck out a brilliant
idea.

Little Sunshine has a cousin Georgy, whom

"THAT'S MAMMA'S PEAR!" SAID SHE.

she is very fond of, and who a few days before had presented her with some pears. These pears had but one fault—they could not be eaten ; being as hard as bullets, and as sour as crabs. They tried the little girl's patience exceedingly, but she was very good. She went every morning to look at them as they stood ranged in a row along mamma's window-sill, and kissed them one by one to make them ripe. At last they did ripen, and were gradually eaten—except one, the biggest and most beautiful of all. " Suppose," mamma suggested, "that we keep it two days more, then it will be quite ripe ; mamma will put it in her pocket, and we will eat it in the train, half-way to Scotland." Little Sunshine looked disappointed, but she did not cry, nor worry mamma — who, she knows, never changes her mind when once she says No—and presently forgot all about it. Until, lo! just as the poor little girl was getting dull and tired, with nothing to do, and nobody to play with, mamma pulled out of her pocket—the identical pear! Such a pear! so large and so pretty—almost too pretty to eat. The child screamed with delight, and immediately began to make public her felicity.

" That's mamma's pear !" said she, touching the coat-sleeve of the old gentleman next her

—a very grim old gentleman—an American, thin and gaunt, with a face not unlike the wolf in Little Red Ridinghood. " That's mamma's pear. Mamma 'membered (remembered) to bring Sunny that pear!"

" Eh ?" said the old gentleman, shaking the little fingers off, not exactly in unkindness, but as if it were a fly that had settled on him and fidgeted him. But Sunny, quite unaccustomed to be shaken off, immediately drew back, shyly and half offended, and did not look at him again.

He went on talking, in a cross and "cantankerous" way, to another gentleman, with a gray beard—an Indian officer, just come from Cashmere, which he declared to be the finest country in the world ; while the American said angrily "that it was nothing like Virginia." But as neither had been in the other country, they were about as able to judge the matter as most people are when they dispute about a thing. Nevertheless, they discussed the question so violently, that Little Sunshine, who is not used to quarrelling, or seeing people quarrel, opened her blue eyes wide with astonishment.

Fortunately, she was engrossed by her pear, which took a long time to eat. First, it had to be pared—in long parings, which twisted and dangled like Sunshine's curls. Then these parings had to be thrown out of the window to the little birds, which were seen sitting here and there on the telegraph wires. Lastly, the pear had to be eaten slowly and deliberately. She fed mamma, herself, and Lizzie too, turn and turn about, in the most conscientious way; uttering at each mouthful that ringing laugh which I wish I could put into paper and print; but I can't. By the time all was done, Sunshine had grown sleepy. She cuddled down in her mamma's arms, with a whispered request for "Maymie's apron."

Now here a confession must be made. The one consolation of life to this little person is the flannel apron upon which her first nurse used to wash her when she was a baby. She takes the two corners of it to stroke her face with one hand, while she sucks the thumb of the other—and so she lies, meditating with open eyes, till at last she goes to sleep. She is never allowed to have the apron in public, so to-day her mamma was obliged to invent a little "Maymie's apron"—a small square of flannel —to comfort her on the long railway journey. This being produced, though she was a little ashamed, and blushed in her pretty childish way, she turned her back on the gentlemen in the carriage and settled down in deep content, her eyes fixed on mamma's face. Gradually they closed—and the lively little woman lay fast asleep, warm and heavy, in her mamma's arms.

There she might have slept till the journey's end, but for those horrid gentlemen, who began to quarrel so fiercely about French and Prussians, and which had the right of it in this terrible war—(a question which you little folks even when you are great big folks fifty years hence may hardly be able to decide)—that they disturbed the poor child in her happy sleep, and at last she started up, looking round her with frightened eyes, and began to scream violently. She had been so good all the way, so little trouble to any body, that mamma could not help thinking it served the gentlemen right, and told them severely that "if gentlemen did differ, they need not do it so angrily as to waken a child." At which they all looked rather ashamed, and were quiet for the rest of the journey.

It did not last much longer; and again the little girl had the fun of jumping out of a puff-puff and into a carriage. The bright day closed; it was already dusk, and pouring rain, and they had to drive a long way, stop at several places, and see several new people whom Little Sunshine had never seen before. She was getting tired and hungry; but still kept good and did not cry; and when at last she came to the cottage which her mamma had told her about, where lived an old gentleman and lady who had been very kind to mamma, and dear grandmamma too, for many years, and would be very kind to the little girl, Sunny ran in at once, as merry as possible.

After a while mamma followed, and lo! there was Little Sunshine, quite at home already, sitting in the middle of the white sheepskin hearth-rug, having taken half her "things" off, chattering in the most friendly manner, and asking to be lifted up to see "a dear little baby and a mamma," which was a portrait of the old lady's eldest sister as an infant in her mother's arms, about seventy years ago.

And what do you think happened next? Sunny actually sat up to supper, which she had never done in all her life before—supper by candle-light: a mouthful of fowl, and a good many mouthfuls of delicious cream, poured, with a tiny bit of jam in the middle of it, into her saucer. And she made a large piece of dry toast into "fishes," and swam them in her mamma's tea, and then fished them out with a teaspoon, and ate them up. Altogether it was a wonderful meal, and left her almost too wide awake to go to bed, if she had not had the delight of sleeping in her mamma's room instead of a nursery, and being bathed, instead of in her own proper bath, in a washing-tub!

This washing-tub was charming. She eyed it doubtfully, she walked round it, she peered over it; at last she slowly got into it.

"Come and see me in my bath; come and see Sunny in her bath," cried she, inviting all the family, half of whom accepted the invitation. Mamma heard such shouts of laughing, with her little girl's laugh clearer than all, that she was obliged to go up stairs to see what was the matter. There was Sunshine frolicking about and splashing like a large fish in the tub, the maids and mistresses standing round, exceedingly amused at their new plaything, the little " water-baby."

But at last the day's excitement was over, and Sunny lay in her white night-gown, cuddled up like a round ball in her mamma's lap, sucking her Maymie's apron, and listening to the adventures of Tommy Tinker. Tommy Tinker is a young gentleman about whom a story, "a quite new story, which Sunny never heard before," has to be told every night.

Mamma had done this for two months, till Tommy, his donkey, his father, John Tinker, who went about the country crying "Pots and kettles to mend," his school-fellow, Jack, and his playfellow, Mary, were familiar characters, and had gone through so much that mamma was often puzzled as to what should happen to them next; this night especially, when she herself was rather tired, but fortunately the little girl grew sleepy very soon.

So she said her short prayers, ending with "God make Sunny a good little girl" (to which she sometimes deprecatingly adds, "but Sunny is a good girl"), curled down in the beautiful large strange bed—such a change from her little crib at home—and was fast asleep in no time.

Thus ended the first day of Little Sunshine's Holiday.

C

CHAPTER II.

NEXT morning Little Sunshine was awake very early, sitting upright in bed, and trying to poke open her mamma's eyes; then she looked about her in the new room with the greatest curiosity.

"There's my tub! there's Sunny's tub! I want to go into my tub again!" she suddenly cried with a shout of delight, and insisted on pattering over to it on her bare feet, and swimming all sorts of things in it—a comb, a brush, biscuits, the soap-dish and soap, and a large penny, which she had found. These kept her amused till she was ready to be dressed, after which she went independently down stairs, where her mamma found her, as before, sitting on the white rug, and conversing cheerfully with the old gentleman and lady, and the rest of the family.

After breakfast she was taken into the garden. It was a very nice garden, with lots of apple-trees in it, and many apples had fallen to the ground. Sunshine picked them up and brought them in her pinafore, to ask mamma if she might eat them—for she never eats any thing without saying, "May I?" and when it is given to her she always says, "Thank you."

Then she went back into the garden again, and saw no end of curious things. Every body was so kind to her, and petted her as if there had never been a child in the house before, which certainly there had not for a great many years. She and her mamma would willingly have staid ever so much longer in the dear little cottage, but there was another house in Scotland, where were waiting Sunshine's two aunties; not real aunties, for she has none, nor uncles neither; but she is a child so well loved, that she has heaps of adopted aunts and uncles too. These—Auntie Weirie and Auntie Maggie—with other kind friends, expected her without fail that very night.

So Sunny was obliged to say good-bye, and start again, which she did on her own two little feet, for the fly forgot to come; and her mamma, and her Lizzie, and two more kind people, had to make a rush of more than a mile, or they would have missed the train. If papa, or any body at home, had seen them—half walking, and half running—and carrying the little girl by turns, or making her run between

them, till she said mournfully, "Sunny can't
run—Sunny is so tired!"—how sorry they
would have been!

And when at the station she lost her mamma, who was busy about luggage, poor Sunny's
troubles seemed great indeed. She screamed
till mamma heard her ever so far off, and when
she caught sight of her again, she clung round
her neck in the most frantic way. "I thought
you was lost; I thought you was lost."

(Sunny's grammar is not perfect yet. She
can not understand tenses; she says "brang"
instead of "brought," and once being told that
this was not right, she altered it to "I brung,"
which, indeed, had some sense, for do we not
say "I rang," and "I rung?" Perhaps Little
Sunshine will yet write a book on grammar—
who knows?)

Well, she parted from her friends, quite
cheerfully of course—she never cries after any
body but her mamma and papa—and soon
made acquaintance with her fellow-travellers,
who this time were chiefly ladies. It being
nearly one o'clock, two of them took a beautiful basket of lunch; sandwiches, and cakes, and
grapes. Little Sunshine watched it with grave
composure until she saw the grapes, which
were very fine. Then she could not help

whispering to her mamma very softly, "Sunny likes grapes."

"Hush!" said mamma, also in a whisper, "They are not ours, so we can't have them"— an answer which always satisfies this little girl. She said no more. But perhaps the young lady who was eating the grapes saw the silent, wistful eyes, for she picked off the most beautiful half of the bunch and handed it over. "Thank you," said Sunny, in the politest way. "Look, mamma! grapes!—shall I give you one?" And the delight of eating them, and feeding mamma with them, "like a little bird," altogether comforted her for the troubles with which she began her journey.

Then she grew conversational, and informed every body that Sunny was going to Scotland, to a place where she had never been before, and that she was to row in a boat and catch big salmon—which no doubt interested them much. She herself was so interested in every thing she saw, that it was impossible not to share her enjoyment. She sat or stood at the carriage window and watched the view. It was quite different from any thing she had been used to. Sunny lives in a very pretty but rather level country, full of woods and lanes, and hedges and fields; but she had nev-

er seen a hill or a river, or indeed (except the
Thames) any sort of water bigger than a horse-
pond. Mamma had sometimes shown her pictures of mountains and lakes, but doubted if
the child had taken it in, and was therefore
quite surprised when she called out, all of a
sudden, "There's a mountain!"

And a mountain it really was—one of those
Westmoreland hills, bleak and bare, which
gradually rise up before travellers' eyes on the
North journey, a foretaste of all the beautiful
things that are coming. Mamma, delighted,
held up her little girl to look at it—the first
mountain Sunny ever saw—with its long,
smooth slopes, and the sheep feeding on them,
dotted here and there like white stones, or moving about like walking daisies.

Little Sunshine was greatly charmed with
the "baa-lambs." She had seen plenty this
spring—white baa-lambs and black baa-lambs,
and white baa-lambs with black faces—but
never so many at a time. And they skipped
about in such a lively way, and stood so fun-
nily in steep places, with their four little legs
all screwed up together, looking at the train
as it passed, that she grew quite excited, and
wanted to jump out and play with him.

To quiet her, mamma told her a story about

the mountains, how curious they looked in winter, all covered with snow; and how the lambs were sometimes lost in the snow, and the shepherds went out to find them, and carried them home in their arms, and warmed them by the fireside and fed them, until they opened their eyes, and stretched their little frozen legs, and began to run about the floor.

Little Sunshine listened, with her wide blue eyes fixed on the mountain, and then upon her mamma's face, never saying a word, till at length she burst out quite breathless, for she does not yet know words enough to get out her thoughts, with—

"I want a little baa-lamb. No"—she stopped and corrected herself—"I want two little baa-lambs. I would go and fetch them in out of the snow, and carry them in my little arms, and lay them on Maymie's apron by my nursery fire, and warm them, and make them quite well again. And the two dear little baa-lambs would play about together—so pretty."

It was a long speech—the longest she had ever made all at once—and the little girl's eyes sparkled and her cheeks grew hot, with the difficulty she had in getting it out, so that mamma might understand. But mamma understands a good deal. Only it was less easy to explain

to Sunny that she could neither have a lamb to
play with, nor go out on the mountain to fetch
it. However, mamma promised that if ever a
little lamb were lost in the snow near her own
house, and her gardener were to find it, he
should be allowed to bring it in, and Sunny
should make it warm by the fire and be kind
to it, until it was quite well again.

But still the child went back now and then
to the matter in a melancholy voice. "I don't
like a dear little baa-lamb to be lost in the snow.
I want a little baa-lamb in my nursery. I
would cuddle it and take such care of it" (for
the strongest instinct of this little woman is to
"take care" of people). "Mamma, some day
may Sunny have a little baa-lamb to take care
of?"

Mamma promised; for she knew well that
if Sunny grows up to be a woman, with the
same instinct of protection that she has now,
God may send her many of His forlorn
"lambs" to take care of.

Presently the baa-lambs were forgotten in a
new sight—a stream; a real, flowing, tumbling
stream—which ran alongside of the railway for
ever so far. It jumped over rocks, and made
itself into white foamy whirlpools, it looked so
very much alive; and so unlike any water that

Sunny had ever seen before, that she was quite astonished.

"What's that?—what's that?" she kept saying; and at last, struck with a sudden idea: "Is it Scotland?"

What her notion of Scotland was—whether a place, or a person, or a thing—her mamma could not make out, but the name was firmly fixed in her mind, and she recurred to it constantly. All the long weary journey, lasting till long after her proper bed-time, she never cried or fretted, or worried any body, but amused herself without ceasing at what she saw. She ate her dinner merrily—"such a funny dinner—no plates, no forks, no table-cloth"—and her tea—milk drank out of a horn cup, instead of "great-grandpapa's mug, which he had when he was a little boy"—which she used when at home.

As the day closed in, she grew tired of looking out of the window, snuggled up in her mamma's arms, and, turning her back upon the people in the carriage, whispered, blushing very much: "Maymie's apron—Sunny wants the little Maymie's apron;" and lay sucking it meditatively, till she dropped asleep.

She was asleep when the train reached Scotland. She did not see the stars coming out

over the Grampian Hills, nor the beautiful fires
near Gartsherrie—that ring of iron furnaces,
blazing fiercely into the night—which are such a
wonderful sight to behold. And she only woke
up in time to have her hat and cloak put on,
and be told that she was really in Scotland,
and would see her aunties in a minute more.
And, sure enough, in the midst of the bustle
and confusion, there was Auntie Weirie's
bright face at the carriage-door, with her arms
stretched out to receive the sleepy little traveller.

Four or five miles were yet to be accomplished, but it was in a comfortable carriage,
dark and quiet. The little girl's tongue was
altogether silent—but she was not asleep, for
all of a sudden she burst out, as if she had been
thinking over the matter for a long time:
"Mamma, you forgot the tickets."

Every body laughed; and mamma explained
to her most accurate little daughter that she
had given up the tickets while Sunny was
asleep. Auntie Weirie foreboded merrily how
Sunny would " keep mamma in order" by-
and-by.

Very sleepy and tired the poor child was;
but, except one entreaty for " a little drop of
milk"—which somehow was got at—she made

no complaint, and never once cried, till the carriage stopped at the house-door.

Oh, such a door, and such a house! Quite a fairy palace! And there, standing waiting, was a pretty lady—not unlike a fairy lady— who took Little Sunshine in her arms and carried her off, unresisting, to a beautiful drawing-room, where, in the great tall mirrors, she could see herself everywhere at full length.

What a funny figure she was, trotting about and examining every thing, as she always does on entering a strange room! Her little water-proof cloak made her look as broad as she was long; and when she tossed off her hat, her curls tumbled about in disorder; and her face and hands were so dirty, that mamma was quite ashamed. But nobody minded it, and every body welcomed her, and the pretty lady carried her off again up stairs into the most charming extempore nursery, next to her mamma's room, where she could run in and out, and be as happy as a queen.

She was as happy as a queen, when she woke up next morning to all the wonders of the house. First there was a poll-parrot, who could say not only "Pretty Poll!" but a great many other words: could bark like a dog, grunt like a pig, and do all sorts of wonderful

things. He lived chiefly in the butler's pantry,
but was brought out on occasion for the amusement of visitors. Sunny was taken to see him
directly; and there she stood, watching him
intently; laughing sometimes in her sudden,
ecstatic way, with her head thrown back, and
her little nose all crumpled up; till, being only
a button of a nose at best, it nearly disappeared
altogether.

And then, in the breakfast-room, there were
two dogs—Jack, a young rough Scotch terrier,
and Bob, a smooth terrier, very ugly and old.
Now Sunny's dog at home, Rose, who was a
puppy when she was a baby, so that the two
were brought up together, is the gentlest creature imaginable. She will let Sunny roll over
her, and pull her paws and tail, and even put
her little fat hand into her mouth, without
growling or biting. But these strange dogs
were not used to children. Sunny tried to
make friends with them, as she tries to do with
every live creature she sees; even crying, one
day, because she could not manage to kiss a
spider, it ran away so fast. But Bob and Jack
did not understand her affection at all. When
she stroked and patted them, and vainly tried
to carry them in her arms, by the legs, head,
tail, or any where she could catch hold of, they

escaped away, scampering off as fast as they
could. The little girl looked after them with
mournful eyes; it was hard to see them frolicking about, and not taking the least notice of her.

But very soon somebody much better than
a little dog began to notice her—a kind boy
named Franky, who, though he was a school-
boy, home for the holidays, did not think it in
the least beneath his dignity to be good to a
little girl. She sat beside him at prayers, during which time she watched him carefully,
and evidently made up her mind that he was
a nice person, and one to be played with. So
when he began playing with her, she responded
eagerly, and they were soon the best of friends.

Presently Franky had to leave her and go
with his big brother down to the bottom of a
coal mine, about which he had told such wonderful stories, that Little Sunshine, had she
been bigger, would certainly have liked to go
too. "You jump into a basket, and are let
down, down, several hundred feet, till you touch
the bottom, and then you find a new world un-
der-ground: long passages, so narrow that you
can not stand upright, and loftier rooms between, and men working—as black as the coal
themselves—with lights in their caps. Also
horses, dragging trucks full of coal—horses

that have never seen the daylight since they were taken down the pit, perhaps seven or ten years ago, and will never see daylight again as long as they live. Yet they live happily, are kindly treated, and have comfortable stables, all in the dark of the coal mine—and no doubt are quite as content as the horses that work in the outside world, high above their heads."

Sunshine heard all this. I can not say that she understood it, being such a very little girl, you know; but whenever Franky opened his lips she watched him with intense admiration, and when he was gone she looked quite sad. However, she soon found another friend in the pretty lady, Franky's mamma. Her own mamma was obliged to go out directly after breakfast, so this other mamma took Sunny under her especial protection, and showed her all about the house. First, they visited the parrot, who went through all his performances over again. Then they proceeded up stairs to what used to be the nursery, only the little girls had grown into big girls, and were now far away at school. But their mamma showed Sunny their old toy-cupboard, where were arranged, in beautiful order, playthings so lovely that it was utterly impossible such very tiny fingers could safely be trusted with them.

So Little Sunshine was obliged to practise the lesson she has learnt with her mamma's china cabinet at home—"Look and not touch." Ever since she was a baby, Wedgwood ware, Sèvres and Dresden china, all sorts of delicate and precious things, have been left within her reach on open shelves; but she was taught from the first that she must not touch them, and she never does. "The things that Sunny *may* play with," such as a small plaster hand, a bronze angel, and a large agate seal, she takes carefully out from among the rest, and is content with them—just as content as she was with one particular doll which the pretty lady chose out from among these countless treasures and gave to her to play with.

Now Sunny has had a good many dolls— wooden dolls, gutta-percha dolls, dolls made of linen with faces of wax—but none of them had ever lasted, entire, for more than twenty-four hours. They always met with some misfortune or other—lost a leg or an arm ; their heads dropped off, and the sawdust ran out of their bodies, leaving them mere empty bits of calico, not dolls at all. The wrecks she had left behind her at home—bodies without heads, heads without bodies, arms and legs sewed upon bodies that did not belong to them, or

strewed about separately in all directions—
would have been melancholy to think of, only
that she loved them quite as well in that dis-
membered condition as when they were new.

But this *was* a dolly—such a dolly as Sunny
had never had before. Perfectly whole, with a
pretty waxen face, a nose, and two eyes; also
hair, real hair that could be combed. This she
at once proceeded to do with her mamma's
comb, just as her Lizzie did her own hair every
morning, until the comb became full of long
flaxen hairs — certainly not mamma's — and
there grew a large bald place on the top of
dolly's head, which Sunny did not understand
at all. Thereupon her Lizzie came to the
rescue, and proposed tying up the poor rem-
nant of curls with a blue ribbon, and dressing
dolly, whose clothes took off and on beautifully, in her out-of-doors dress, so that Sunshine
might take her a walk in the garden.

Lizzie is a very ingenious person in mending
and dressing dollies, and has also the gift of
unlimited patience with her charge; so the
toilet went off very well, and soon both Sunshine and her doll were ready to go out with
Franky's mamma and see the cows, pigs, sheep,
chickens, and all the wonders of the outside establishment, which was a very large one.

Indeed the pretty lady showed her so many curious things, and played with her so much, that when, just before dark, her own mamma came back, and saw a little roly-poly figure, hugging a large doll, running as fast as ever it could along the gravel-walk to meet her—she felt convinced that the first day in Scotland had been a most delightful one, altogether perfect in its way. So much so that, when put to bed, Sunny again forgot Tommy Tinker. She was chattering so much of all she had seen, that it was not until the last minute that she remembered to ask for a "story."

There was no story in mamma's head to-night.. Instead, she told something really true, which had happened in the street near the house where she had spent the day :—

A poor little boy, just come out of school, was standing on the top of the school-door steps, with his books in his hand. Suddenly a horse that was passing took fright, rushed up the steps, and knocked the boy down. He fell several feet, and a huge stone fell after, just on the top of him—and—and—

Mamma stopped. She could not tell any more of the pitiful story. Her child's eyes were fixed upon her face, which Little Sunny reads sometimes as plain as any book.

D

" Mamma, was the poor little boy hurt ?"

" Yes, my darling."

" Very much hurt ?"

" Very much, indeed."

Sunny sat upright, and began speaking loud and fast, in her impetuous, broken way.

" I want to go and see that poor little boy. I will bring him to my nursery and put him in my little bed, and take care of him. Then he will get quite well."

And she looked much disappointed when her mamma explained that this was not necessary; somebody having already carried the little boy home to his mamma.

" Then his mamma will cuddle him, and kiss the sore place, and he will be quite well soon. Is he quite well ?"

" Yes," answered Sunny's mamma, after a minute's thought—" yes, he is quite well now; nothing will ever hurt him any more."

Sunny was perfectly satisfied.

But her mamma, when she kissed the little curly head, and laid it down on its safe pillow, thought of that other mother—mourning over a dead child — thoughts which Little Sunshine could not understand, nor was there any need she should. She may, some day, when she has a little girl of her own.

CHAPTER III.

L ITTLE SUNSHINE had never yet beheld the sea. That wonderful delight, a sea-beach, with little waves running in and running back again, playing at bo-peep among shingle and rocks, or a long smooth sandy shore, where you may pick up shells and seaweed and pebbles, and all sorts of curious things, and build castles and dig moats, filled with real water—all this was unknown to the little girl. So her mamma, going to spend a day with a dear old friend, who lived at a lovely sea-side house, thought she would take the child with her. Also "the big child;" as her Sunny sometimes called Lizzie, who enjoyed going about and seeing new places as much as the little child.

They started directly after breakfast one morning, leaving behind them the parrot, the dogs, and every thing except Franky, who escorted them in the carriage through four or five miles of ugly town streets, where all the little children who ran about (and there seemed

no end of them) had very rough bare heads,
and very dirty bare feet.

Sunny was greatly struck by them.

"Look, mamma, that little boy has got no
shoes and stockings on! Shall Sunny take off
hers and give them to that poor little boy?"

And she was proceeding to unbutton her
shoes, when her mamma explained that—the
boy being quite a big boy—Sunny's shoes
would certainly not fit him, and if they did, he
would probably not put them on; since in
Scotland little boys and girls often go barefooted, and like it. Had not papa once taken
off Sunny's shoes and stockings, and let her
run about upon the soft warm grass of the
lawn, calling her "his little Scotch girl?"

Sunny accepted the reasoning, but still looked perplexed at the bare feet. They were
"so dirty," and she can not bear to have the
least speck of dirt on feet or hands or clothes,
or anywhere about her. Her Auntie Weirie,
on whose lap she sat, and of whom she had
taken entire possession—children always do—
was very much amused.

She put them safely into the train, which
soon started—on a journey which mamma
knew well, but which seemed altogether fresh
when seen through her child's eyes. Such

wonderful things for Sunshine to look at!
Mountains—she thoroughly understood mountains now; and a broad river, gradually growing broader still, until it was almost sea. Ships
too—some with sails, and some with chimneys
smoking; "a puff-puff on the water," Sunny
called them. Every now and then there was
a little "puff-puff" dragging a big ship after
it, and going so fast, fast—the big ship looking
as proud as if it were sailing along all by its
own self, and the little one puffing and blowing
as busily as possible. Sunny watched them
with much curiosity, and then started a brilliant idea.

"That's a papa-boat and that's a baby-boat,
and the baby-boat pulls the papa-boat along!
So funny!"

And she crumpled up her little face, and,
tossing up her head, laughed her quite inde-
scribable laugh, which makes every body else
laugh too.

There were various other curious things to
be seen on the river, especially some things
which mamma told her were called "buoys."
These of course she took to mean little "boys,"
and looked puzzled, until mamma described
them as "big red thimbles," which she understood, and noticed each one with great interest
ever afterwards.

But it would be vain to tell all the things she saw, and all the delight she took in them. Occasionally her little face grew quite grave, such difficulty had she in understanding the wonders that increased more and more. And when at last the journey was ended and the train. stopped, the little girl was rather troubled, and would not let go of her mamma for a single minute.

For the lovely autumn weather of yesterday had changed into an equinoctial gale. Inland, one did not so much perceive it, but at the seaside it was terrible. People living on that coast will long remember this particular day as one of the wildest of the season, or for several seasons. The wind blew, and the sea roared, as even mamma, who knew the place well, had seldom heard. Instead of tiny wavelet's running after Sunny's little feet, as had been promised her, there were huge "white horses" rising and falling in the middle of the river; while along the shore the waves kept pouring in, and dashing themselves in and out of the rocks, with force enough to knock any poor little girl down. Sunny could not go·· near them, and the wind was so high that her hat had to be tied on; and her cloak, a cape of violet wool, which Auntie Weirie had rushed to fetch at the last minute, in case of rain, was the greatest possible blessing. Still, fasten it as Lizzie would, the wind blew it loose again, and tossed her curls all over her face in a furious fashion, which the little girl could not understand at all.

"Sunny don't like it," said she, pitifully; and, forgetful of all the promised delights—shells, and pebbles, and castles of sand—took refuge gladly in-doors.

However, this little girl is of such a happy nature in herself that she quickly grows happy anywhere. And the house she came to was such a beautiful house, with a conservatory full of flowers—she is so fond of flowers—and a large hall to play in besides. Her merry voice was soon heard in all directions, rather to her mamma's distress, as the dear mistress of the house was not well. But Sunny comprehends that she must always speak in a whisper when people are not well; so she was presently quieted down, and came into the dining-room and ate her dinner by mamma's side, as good as gold. She has always dined with mamma ever since she could sit up in a chair, so she behaves quite properly—almost like a grown-up person. When she and mamma are alone, they converse all dinner-time; but when there are other people present, she is told that "little girls must be seen and not heard"—a rule which she observes as far as she can. Not altogether, I am afraid, for she is very fond of talking.

Still she was good, upon the whole, and enjoyed herself much, until she had her things put on again, ready to start once more, in a kind lady's carriage which was ordered to drive slowly along the shore, that Sunny might see as much as possible, without being exposed to the wind and spray. She was much interested, and a little awed. She ceased to chatter, and sat looking out of the carriage window on the curve of shore, over which the tide came pouring in long rollers, and sweeping back again in wide sheets of water mixed with white foam.

"Does Sunny like the waves?" asked the kind lady, who has a sweet way with children, and is very good to them, though she has none of her own.

"Yes, Sunny likes them," said the little girl, after a pause, as if she were trying to make up her mind. 'Posing (supposing) Sunny were to go and swim upon them? If—if mamma would come too?"

"But wouldn't Sunny be afraid?"

"No"—very decidedly this time. "Sunny would be quite safe if mamma came too."

The lady smiled at mamma; who listened, scarcely smiling, and did not say a word.

It was a terrible day. The boats, and even big ships, were tossing about like cockle-shells on the gray stormy sea; and the mountains, hiding themselves in mist, at last altogether disappeared. Then the rain began to fall in sheets, as it often does fall hereabouts—soaking, blinding rain. At the station it was hardly possible to keep one's footing: the little girl, if she had not been in her Lizzie's arms, would certainly have been blown down before she got into the railway carriage.

Once there—safely sheltered from the storm—she did not mind it in the least. She jumped about, and played endless tricks, to the great amusement of two ladies—evidently a mamma and a grandmamma—who compared her with their own little people, and were very kind to her—as indeed every body is when she travels. Still, even they might have got tired out, if Sunny had not fortunately grown tired herself, and began to yawn in the midst of her fun in a droll way.

Then mamma slyly produced out of her pocket the child's best travelling companion—

the little Maymie's apron. Sunny seized it
with a scream of delight, cuddled down, sucking it, in her mamma's arms, and in three minutes was sound asleep. Nor did she once
wake up till the train stopped, and Lizzie carried her, so muffled up that nobody could have
told whether it was a little girl or a brown
paper parcel, to the carriage, where faithful
Franky waited for her, and had waited ever
so long.

Fun and Franky always came together.
Sunny shook herself wide awake at once—
fresh as a rose, and lively as a kitten. Oh the
games that began, and lasted all the four miles
that the carriage drove through the pelting
rain! Never was a big boy kinder to a little
girl; so patient, so considerate; letting her do
any thing she liked with him; never cross,
and never rough—in short, a thorough gentleman, as all boys should be to all girls, and all
men to all women, whether old or young.
And when home was reached, the fire, like the
welcome, was so warm and bright that Sunny
seemed to have lost all memory of her day at
the sea-side—the stormy waves, the dreary
shore, the wild wind, and pouring rain. She
was such a contented little girl that she never
heeded the weather outside. But her mamma

did a little, and thought of sailors at sea, and soldiers fighting abroad, and many other things.

The happy visit was now drawing to a close. Perhaps as well, lest, as some people foretold, Sunny might get "quite spoiled"—if love spoils any body, which I do not believe. Certainly this child's felicities were endless. Every body played with her; every body was kind to her. Franky and Franky's mamma, her two aunties, the parrot, the dogs Bob and Jack, were her companions by turns. There was another dog, Wallace by name : but she did not play with him, as he was an older and graver and bigger animal—much bigger than herself indeed. She once faintly suggested riding him, "as if he was a pony," but the idea was not caught at, and fell to the ground, as, doubtless, Sunny would have done immediately, had she carried out her wish.

Wallace, though big, was the gentlest dog imaginable. He was a black retriever, belonging to Franky's elder brother, a grown-up young gentleman ; and his devotion to his master was entire. The rest of the family he just condescended to notice—but Mr. John he followed everywhere with a quiet persistency— the more touching because poor Wallace was nearly blind. He had lost the sight of one eye

by an accident, and could see out of the other
very little. They knew how little, by the near
chance he had often had of being run over by
other carriages in following theirs; so that now
Franky's mamma never ventured to take him
out with her at all. He was kept away from
streets, but allowed to run up and down in the
country, where his wonderful sense of smell
preserved him from any great danger.   ·

This sense of smell, common to all retrievers,
seemed to have been doubled by Wallace's
blindness. He could track his master for miles
and miles, and find any thing that his master
had touched. Once, just to try him, Mr. John
showed him a halfpenny, and then hid it under
a tuft of grass, and walked on across country ·
for half a mile or more. Of course the dog
could not *see* where he hid it, and had been
galloping about in all directions ever since;
yet when his master said, " Wallace, fetch that
halfpenny," showing him another one, Wallace
instantly turned back, smelling cautiously about
for twenty yards or so; then, having caught
the right scent, bounding on faster and faster,
till out of sight. In half an hour more he
came back, and ran direct to his master with
the halfpenny in his mouth.

Since, Mr. John had sent the dog for his

stick, his cap, or his handkerchief, often considerable distances; but Wallace always brought the thing safe back, whatever it was, and laid it at his master's feet. Mr. John was very proud of Wallace, and very fond of him.

Sunny was not old enough to understand these clevernesses of the creature, but she fully appreciated one trick of his. He would hold a bit of biscuit or sugar on his nose, quite steady, for several minutes, while his master said "Trust," not attempting to eat it; but when Mr. John said "Paid for!" Wallace gobbled it up at once. This he did several times, to Sunshine's great delight, but always with a sort of hesitation, as if he considered it a little below the dignity of such a very superior animal. And the minute they were gone he would march away with his slow blind step, following his beloved master.

But all pleasures come to an end, and so did these of Little Sunshine's. First, Franky went off to school, and she missed him out of the house very much. Then one day, instead of the regular morning amusements, she had to be dressed quickly, to eat her breakfast twice as fast as usual, and have her "things" put on all in a hurry "to go by the puff-puff." Her only consolation was that Dolly should have her things put on too—poor Dolly ! who, from constant combing, was growing balder and balder every day, and whose clothes were slowly disappearing, so that it required all Lizzie's ingenuity to dress her decently for the journey.

This done, Sunny took her in her arms, and became so absorbed in her as hardly to notice the affectionate adieux of her kind friends, some of whom went with her to the station : so she scarcely understood that it was good-bye. And besides, it is only elder folks who understand good-byes, not little people.   All the better, too.

Sunshine was delighted to be in a puff-puff again; and to see more mountains.   She watched them till she was tired, and then went comfortably to sleep, having first made Dolly comfortable too, lying as snug in her arms as she did in her mamma's.   But she and Dolly woke up at the journey's end ; when, indeed, Sunny became so energetic and lively, that seeing her mamma and her Lizzie carrying each a bag, she insisted on carrying something too.   Seizing upon a large luncheon basket which the pretty lady had filled with no end of good things, she actually lifted it, and bore it, tottering under its weight, for several yards.

" See, mamma, Sunny *can* carry it," said she

in triumph, and her mamma never hinders the little girl from doing every thing she *can* do; wishing to make her a useful and helpful woman, who will never ask any body else to do for her what she can do for herself.

The place they were going to was quite different from that they had left. It was only lodgings—in a house on the top of a hill—but they were nice lodgings, and it was a bright breezy hill, sloping down to a beautiful glen, through which ran an equally beautiful stream. Thence, the country sloped up again, through woods and pasture-lands, to a dim range of mountains, far in the horizon. A very pretty place outside, and not bad inside, only the little girl's " nursery " was not so large and cheerful as the one she was used to, and she missed the full house and the merry companions. However, being told that papa was coming to-morrow, she brightened up, and informed every body, whether interested or not in the fact, that " Sunny was going to see papa jump out of a puff-puff, to-morrow." " To-morrow" being still to her a very indefinite thing ; but " papa jumping out of a puff-puff" has long been one of the great features of her existence.

Still, to-day she would have been rather dull, if when she went out into the garden there had

not come timidly forward, to look at her, a little girl, whose name mamma inquired, and
found that it was Nelly.

Here a word or two ought to be said about
Nelly, for she turned out the greatest comfort
to solitary little Sunny, in this strange place.
Nelly was not exactly "a young lady;" indeed
at first she hung back in a sweet shy way, as
doubtful whether Sunny's mamma would allow the child to play with her. But Nelly
was such a good little girl, so well brought-up
and sensible, though only ten years old, that
a princess might have had her for a playfellow without any disadvantage. And as soon
as mamma felt sure that Sunny would learn
nothing bad from her—which is the only real
objection to playfellows—she allowed the children to be together as much as ever they
liked.

Nelly called Sunshine "a bonnie wee lassie"
—words which, not understanding what they
meant, had already offended her several times
since she came to Scotland.

"I'm not a bonnie wee lassie—I'm Sunny;
mamma's little Sunny, I am!" cried she, almost
in tears. But this was the only annoyance
that Nellie ever gave her.

Very soon the two children were sitting to-

gether in a most charming play-place—some
tumble-down, moss-grown stone steps leading
down to the garden. From thence you could
see the country for miles, and watch the railway trains winding along like big serpents,
with long feathers of steam and smoke stream-
ing from their heads in the daylight, and great
red fiery eyes gleaming through the dark.

Nelly had several stories to tell about them
—how once a train caught fire, and blazed up
—they saw the blaze from these steps—and
very dreadful it was to look at; also, she
wanted to know if Sunny had seen the river
below ; such a beautiful little river, only sometimes people were drowned in it—two young
ladies who were bathing, and also a school-
master, who had fallen into a deep hole, which
was now called the Dominie's Hole.

Nelly spoke broad Scotch, but her words
were well chosen, and her manner very simple
and gentle and sweet. She had evidently
been carefully educated, as almost all Scotch
children are. She went to school, she said,
every morning, so that she could only play
with Sunny of afternoons; but to-morrow afternoon, if the lady allowed—there was still
that pretty polite hesitation at any thing that
looked like intrusiveness—she would take Sun-

E

ny and her Lizzie a walk, and show them all
that was to be seen.

Sunny's mamma not only allowed this—but
was glad of it. Little Nelly seemed a rather
grave and lonely child. She had no brothers
and sisters, she said, but lived with her aunts,
who were evidently careful over her. She
was a useful little body ; went many a mes-
sage to the village, and did various things
about the house, as a girl of ten can often do ;
but she was always neatly dressed, her hands
and face quite clean, and her pretty brown
hair, the chief prettiness she had, well combed
and brushed. And, above all, she never said
a rude or ugly word.

It was curious to see how Little Sunshine,
who, though not shy or repellent, is never affectionate to strangers, and always declines ca-
resses, saying "she only kisses papa and mamma," accepted Nelly's kiss almost immediately, and allowed her to make friends at once.
Nay, when bed-time arrived, she even invited
her to "come and see Sunny in her bath," a
compliment she only pays occasionally to her
chief favorites. Soon the two solitary children were frolicking together, and the gloomy
little nursery—made up extempore out of a
back bedroom—ringing with their laughter.

At last, fairly tired with her day's doings, Sunny condescended to go to sleep. Her mamma sat up for an hour or two longer, writing letters, and listening to the child's soft breathing through the open door, to the equally soft sough of the wind outside, and the faint murmur of the stream, deep below in the glen. Then she also went to rest.

CHAPTER IV.

NELLY turned out more and more of an acquisition every day. Pretty as this new place was, Little Sunshine was not quite so happy as the week before. She had not so many things to amuse her out-of-doors; and in-doors she was kept more to her nursery than she approved of or was accustomed to, being in her own home mamma's little friend and companion all day long. Now mamma was often too busy to attend to her, and had to slip away and hide out of sight; for whenever Sunny caught sight of her, the wail of "Mamma, mamma, I want you!" was really sad to hear.

Besides, she had another tribulation. In the nearest house, a short distance down the lane, lived six children whom she knew and was fond of, and had come to Scotland on purpose to play with. But alas! one of them caught the measles; and, Little Sunshine never having had measles, or any thing—in fact, never having had a day's illness or taken a

dose of physic in her life—the elders decided
that it was best to keep the little folks apart.
Mamma tried hard not to let Sunny find out
that her dear playfellows of old lived so near;
but one day these sharp little ears caught their
names, and from that time she ·was always
wanting to go and play with them, and especially with their " little baby."

"I want to see that little baby, mamma;
may Sunny go and cuddle the dear little
baby?"

But it was the baby which had the measles,
and some of the rest were not safe. So there
was nothing for it but to give orders to each
household that when they saw one another·
they were to ·run away at once; which they
most honorably did. Still it was hard for Sunny to see her little friends—whom she recog-
nized at once, though they had not met for
eight months—galloping about, as merry as
possible, playing at " ponies," and all sorts of
things, while she was kept close to her Lizzie's
side and not allowed to go near them.

Thus, but for kind little Nelly, the child
would have been dull—at least, as dull as such
a sunshiny child could well be—which was not
saying much. If she grows up with her present capacity for enjoying herself, little Sunny

will be a blessing wherever she goes: since happy-minded people always make others happy. Still, Nelly was welcome company, especially of afternoons.

The days passed on very much alike. Before breakfast, Sunny always went a walk with her mamma, holding hands, and talking like two grown-up persons—about the baa-lambs, and calves, and cows, which they met on their way along the hill-side. It was a beautiful hill-side, and every thing looked so peaceful in the early morning. They seldom met any body; except once, when they were spoken to by a funny-looking man, who greatly offended Sunny by asking if she were a boy or girl, but added, "It's a fine bairn, anyhow!" Then he went on to say how he had just come "frae putting John M'Ewen in his coffin, ye ken; I'm gaun to Glasgow, but I'll be back here o' Saturday. Ay, ay, I'll be back o' Saturday;" as if the assurance must be the greatest satisfaction to Sunny and her mamma. Mamma thought he must have been drunk; but no, he was only foolish—a poor half-witted fellow, whom all the neighborhood knew, and were good to. He had some queer points. Among the rest, a most astonishing memory. He would go to church, and then repeat the sermon, or long bits

of it, off by heart, to the first person he met.
Though silly, he was quite capable of taking
care of himself, and never harmed any body.
Every body, Nelly said, was kind to "'daft
John." Still, Sunny did not fancy him; and
when she came home she told her papa a long
story about "that ugly man!"

She had great games with her papa now
and then, and was very happy whenever she
could get hold of him. But her great companion was Nelly. From the minute Nelly came
out of school till seven o'clock—Sunny's bed-
time—they were inseparable; and the way the
big girl devoted herself to the little one, the
patience with which she submitted to all her
vagaries, and allowed herself to be tyrannized
over—never once failing in good-temper and
pleasantness—was quite pretty to see. They
played in the garden together; they went
walks; they gathered blackberries, made them
into jam in a little saucer by the fire, and then
ate them up. With a wooden spade, and a
"luggie" to fill with earth, they used to go up
the hill-side, or down to the glen, sometimes
disappearing for so long that mamma was rather unhappy in her mind, only Nelly was such
a cautious little person, that whenever she went
she was sure to bring her two charges home in
safety.

One day, Nelly not being attainable, mamma went with the "big child" and the little one to the Dominie's Hole.

It was a real long walk, especially for such tiny feet, that eighteen months ago could barely toddle alone: all across the field of the baa-lambs, which always interested Sunny so much that it was difficult to get her past them : she wanted to play with them and "cuddle" them; and was much surprised when they invariably ran away. However, she was to-day a little consoled by mamma's holding her upon the top of the stone dike at the end of the field, to watch "the water running" between the trees of the glen.

In Scotland water runs as I think it never does in England—so loudly and merrily, so fast and bright. Even when it is brown water —as when coming over peat it often is—there is a beauty about it beyond all quiet Southern streams. Here, however, it was not colored, but clear as crystal in every channel of the little river, and it was divided into tiny channels by big stones, and shallow, pebbly water-courses, and overhanging rocks covered with ferns, and heather, and mosses. Beneath these were generally round pools, where the river settled dark and still, though so clear that you could easily see to the bottom, which looked only two or three feet deep, when perhaps it was twelve or fifteen.

The Dominie's Hole was one of these. You descended to it by a winding path through the glen, and then came suddenly out upon a sheltered nook surrounded by rocks, over which the honeysuckles crept, and the birk or mountain ash grew out of every possible cranny. Down one of these rocks the pent-up stream poured in a noisy little waterfall, forming below a deep bathing-pool, cut in the granite—I think it was granite—like a basin, with smooth sides and edges. Into this pool, many years ago, the poor young "Dominie," or school-master, had dived, and striking his head against the bottom, had been stunned and drowned. He was found floating dead, in the lonely little pool, which ever after bore his name.

A rather melancholy place, and the damp, sunless chill of it made it still more gloomy, pretty as it was. Little Sunshine, who can not bear living in shadow, shivered involuntarily, and whispered, "Mamma, take her!" as she always does in any doubtful or dangerous circumstances. So mamma was obliged to carry her across several yards of slippery stones, green with moss, that she might look up to the water-

fall, and down to the Dominie's Hole. She did
not quite like it, evidently, but was not actually frightened — she is such a very courageous person whenever she is in her mamma's
arms.

When set down on her own two feet, the
case was different. She held by her mamma's
gown, looked at the noisy tumbling water with
anxious eyes, and seemed relieved to turn her
back upon it, and watch the half-dozen merry
rivulets into which it soon divided, as they
spread themselves in and out over the shallow
channel of the stream. What charming little
baby rivers they were! Sunny and her mamma could have played among them for hours,
damming them up with pebbles, jumping over
them, floating leaves down them, and listening
to their ceaseless singing, and their dancing too,
with bubbles and foam gliding on their surface
like little fairy boats, till—pop!—all suddenly
vanished, and were seen no more.

It was such a thirsty place, too—until mamma made her hand into a cup for the little girl,
and then the little girl insisted on doing the
same for mamma, which did not answer quite
the same purpose, being so small. At last
mamma took out of her pocket a letter (it was
a sad letter, with a black edge, but the child

did not know that), and made its envelope into
a cup, from which Sunny drank in the greatest delight. Afterwards she administered it to
her mamma and her Lizzie, till the saturated
paper began to yield—its innocent little duty
was done. However, Sunny insisted on filling
it again herself, and was greatly startled when
the bright fierce-running water took it right
out of her hand, whirled it along for a yard or
too, and then sunk it, soaked through, in the
first eddy which the stream reached.

Poor child! she looked after her frail treas-
ure with eyes in which big tears—and Sunny's
tears, when they do come, are so very big!—
were just beginning to rise; and her rosy
mouth fell at the corners, with that pitiful look
mamma knows well, though it is not often
seen.

"Never mind, my darling; mamma will
make her another cup out of the next letter
she has. Or, better still, she will find her own
horn cup, that has been to Scotland so often,
and gone about for weeks in mamma's pocket,
years ago. Now Sunny shall have it to drink
out of."

"And to swim? May Sunny have it to
swim?"

"No, dear, because, though it would not go

down to the bottom like the other cup, it might swim right away and be lost, and then mamma would be so sorry. No, Sunny can't have it to swim, but she may drink out of it as often as she likes. Shall we go home and look for it?"

" Yes."

The exact truth, told in an intelligible and reasonable way, always satisfies this reasonable child, who has been accustomed to have every prohibition explained to her, so far as was possible. Consequently, the sense of injustice, which even very young children have, when it is roused, never troubles her. She knows mamma will give her every thing she can, and when she does not, it is simply because she can't, and she tells Sunny *why* she can't, whenever Sunny can understand it.

So they climbed contentedly up the steep brae, and went home.

Nothing else happened here—at least to the child. If she had a rather dull life, it was a peaceful one. She was out-of-doors a great deal, with Lizzie and Nelly of afternoons, with her mamma of early mornings. Generally, each day, the latter contrived to get a quiet hour or two ; while her child played about the garden steps, and she sat reading the newspa-

per—the terrible newspaper! When Sunny
has grown up a woman, she will know what a
year this year 1870 has been, and understand
how many a time, when her mamma was walking along with her, holding her little hand, and
talking about all the pretty things they saw,
she was thinking of other mothers and other
children, who, instead of running merrily over
sunshiny hill-sides, were weeping over dead
fathers, or dying miserably in burnt villages, or
starving day by day in besieged cities. This
horrible war, brought about, as war almost always is, by a few wicked, ambitious men, made
her feel half frantic.

One day especially—the day the Prussians
came and sat down before Paris, and began
the siege—Little Sunshine was playing about,
with her little wooden spade, and a "luggie"
that her papa had lately bought for her; filling
it with pebbles, and then digging in the garden-
beds, with all her small might. Her mamma
sat on the garden steps, reading the newspaper.
Sunny did not approve of this at all.

"Come and build me a house. Put that
down," pulling at the newspaper, "and build
Sunny a house. Please, mamma," in a very
gentle tone—she knows in a minute by mamma's look when she has spoken too roughly—

"Please, mamma, come and build Sunny a house."

And getting no answer, she looked fixedly at her mamma—then hugged her tight round the neck, and began to sob for sympathy. Poor lamb! She had evidently thought only little girls cried—not mammas at all.

The days ran on fast, fast; and it was time for another move and another change in Little Sunshine's holiday. Of course she did not understand these changes; but she took them cheerfully—she was the very best of little travellers. The repeated packing had ceased to be an interest to her; she never wanted now to jump upon mamma's gowns, and sit down on her bonnets, by way of being useful; but still the prospect of going in a puff-puff was always felicitous. She told Nelly all about it; and how she was afterwards to sail in a boat with Maurice and Maurice's papa (Maurice was a little playfellow, of whom more presently), how they were to go fishing and catch big salmon.

"Wouldn't you like to catch a big salmon?" she asked Nelly, not recognizing in the least that she was parting with her, probably never to meet again in all their lives. But the elder child looked sad and grave during the whole of that day. And when for the last time Nelly put her arms round Sunny, and kissed her over and over again, Sunny being of course just as merry as ever, and quite unconscious that they were bidding one another good-bye, it was rather hard for poor little Nelly.

However, the child did not forget her kind companion. For weeks and even months afterwards, upon hearing the least allusion to this place, Sunshine would wake up into sudden remembrance. "Where's Nelly? I want to see Nelly—I want Nelly to come and play with me;" and look quite disappointed when told that Nelly was far away, and couldn't come. Which was perhaps as much as could be expected of three-years-old.

Always happy in the present, and frightened at nothing so long as she was "close by mamma," Little Sunshine took her next journey. On the way she staid a night at the seaside place where she had been taken before, and this time the weather was kind. She wandered with her Lizzie on the beach, and watched the waves for a long time; then she went in-doors, to play with some other little children, and to pay a visit to the dear old lady who had been ill, when she was here last. Here I am afraid she did not behave quite as

well as she ought to have done—being tired
and sleepy; nor did she half enough value
the kind little presents she got; but she will
some day, and understand the difference between eighty years of age and three, and how
precious to a little child is the blessing of an
old woman. ·

Sunny went to bed rather weary and forlorn, but she woke up next morning and ran
in to papa and mamma, still in her night-
gown, with her little bare feet pattering along
the floor, looking as bright as the sunshine itself. Which was very bright that day—a
great comfort, as there was a ten hours' sea-
voyage before the little woman, who had never been on board a steamboat, and never travelled so long at a time in all her life. She
made a good breakfast to start with, sitting at
table with a lot of grown-up people whose
faces were as blithe as her own, and behaving
very well, considering. Then came another
good-bye, of course unheeded by Little Sunshine, and she was away on her travels once
more.

But what happened to her next must be put
into a new chapter.

CHAPTER V.

THE pier Sunny started from was one near
the mouth of a large estuary or firth,
where a great many ships of all sorts are constantly coming and going. Sometimes the
firth is very stormy, as on the first day when
she was there, but to-day it was smooth as
glass. The mountains round it looked half
asleep in a sunshiny haze, and upon the river
itself was not a single ripple. The steamers
glided up and down in the distance as quietly
as swans upon a lake. You could just catch
the faint click-clack of their paddle-wheels,
and see the long trail of smoke following after
them, till it melted into nothing.

"Where's Sunny's steamboat? Sunny is
going a sail in a steamboat," chattered the little girl; who catches up every thing, sometimes even the longest words and the queerest
phrases, nobody knows how.

Sunny's steamboat lay alongside the pier.
Its engines were puffing and its funnel smoking; and when she came to the gangway she
looked rather frightened, and whispered, "Mam-

F

ma, take her," holding out those pathetic little
arms.

Mamma took her, and from that safe emi-
nence she watched every thing: the men loos-
ing the ropes from the pier, the engines moving, the sea-gulls flying about in little flocks,
almost as tame as pigeons. She was much
amused by these sea-gulls, which always follow the steamers, seeming to know quite well
that after every meal on board they are sure
to get something. She called her Lizzie to
look at them—her Lizzie, who always sym-
pathizes with her in every thing. Now it was
not quite easy, as Lizzie also had never been
on board a steamer before, and did not altogether relish it.

But she, too, soon grew content and happy,
for it was a beautiful scene. There was no distant view, the mountains being all in a mist of
heat, but the air was so bright and mild, with
just enough saltness in it to be refreshing, that
it must have been a very gloomy person who
did not enjoy the day. Little Sunshine did to
the utmost. She could not talk, but became
absorbed in looking about her, endless wonder
at every thing she saw or heard shining in her
blue eyes. Soon she heard something which
brightened them still more.

"Hark, mamma! music! Sunny hears music."

It was a flute played on the lower deck, and played exceedingly well.

Now this little girl has a keen sense of music. Before she could speak, singing always soothed her; and she has long been in the habit of commanding extempore tunes—"a tune that Sunny never heard before," sometimes taking her turn to offer one. "Mamma, shall I sing you a song—a song you never heard before?" (Which certainly mamma never had.) She distinguishes tunes at once, and is very critical over them. "Sunny likes it," or "Sunny don't like it—it isn't pretty;" and at the sound of any sort of music she pricks up her ears, and will begin to cry passionately if not taken to listen.

This flute she went after at once. It was played by a blind man, who stood leaning against the stairs leading to the higher deck, his calm sightless face turned up to the dazzling sunshine. It could not hurt him; he seemed even to enjoy it. There was nobody listening, but he played on quite unconsciously, one Scotch tune after another, the shrill, clear, pure notes floating far over the sea. Sunny crept closer and closer—her eyes grow-

ing larger and larger with intense delight—
till the man stopped playing. Then she whispered,

"Mamma, look at that poor man! Somekin
wrong with his eyes."

Sunny has been taught that whenever there
is "somekin (something) wrong" with any
body—when they are blind, or lame, or ugly,
or queer-looking, we are very sorry for them,
but we never notice it; and so, though she has
friends who can not run about after her, but
walk slowly with a stick, or even two sticks—
also other friends who only feel her little face,
and pass their hands over her hair, saying how
soft it is—mamma is never afraid of her making any remark that could wound their feelings.

"Hush! the poor man can't see, but we
must not say any thing about it. Come with
mamma, and we will give him a penny." All
sorts of money are "pennies" to Sunny—
brown pennies, white pennies, yellow pennies;
only she much prefers the brown pennies, because they are largest, and spin the best.

So she and mamma went up together to the
poor blind man, Sunny looking hard at him;
and he was not pleasant to look at, as his
blindness seemed to have been caused by
small-pox. But the little girl said not a word,

only put the white "penny" into his hand,
and went away.

I wonder whether he felt the touch of those
baby fingers, softer than most. Perhaps he
did, for he began to play again, the "Flowers
of the Forest," with a pathos that even mamma in all her life had never heard excelled.
The familiar mountains, the gleaming river,
the "sunshiny" child, with her earnest face,
and the blind man playing there, in notes that
almost spoke the well-known words,

"Thy frown canna fear me, thy smile canna cheer me,
For the flowers o' the forest are a' wede away."

It was a picture not easily to be forgotten.

Soon the steamer stopped at another pier,
where were waiting a number of people, ready
to embark on a large excursion-boat which all
summer long goes up and down the firth
daily, taking hundreds of passengers, and giving them twelve pleasant hours of sea air and
mountain breezes. She was called the "Iona,"
and such a big boat as she was! She had two
decks, with a saloon below. On the first deck,
the passengers sat in the open air, high up, so
as to see all the views; the second was under
cover, with glass sides, so that they could still
see all about; the third, lower yet, was the

cabin, where they dined. There was a ladies'
cabin, too, where a good many babies and children, with their nurses and mammas, generally staid all the voyage. Altogether, a most
beautiful boat, with plenty of play-places for
little folk, and comfortable nooks for elder
ones; and so big, too, that as she came steaming down the river, she looked as if she could
carry a townful of people. Indeed, this summer, when nobody has travelled abroad, owing
to the war, the "Iona" had carried regularly
several hundreds a day.

Sunny gazed with some amazement from the
pier, where she had disembarked, in her mamma's arms. It is fortunate for Sunny that she
has a rather tall mamma, so that she feels safely
elevated above any crowd. This was a crowd
such as she had never been in before; it jos-
tled and pushed her, and she had to hold very
tight round her mamma's neck; so great was
the confusion, and so difficult the passage across
the gangway to the deck of the "Iona." Once
there, however, she was as safe and happy as
possible, playing all sorts of merry tricks, and
wandering about the boat in all directions,
with her papa, or her Lizzie, or two young ladies who came with her, and were very kind
to her. But after a while these quitted the

boat, and were watched climbing up a mountain-side as cleverly as if they had been young deer. Sunny would have liked to climb a mountain too, and mamma promised her she should some day.

She was now in the very heart of the Highlands. There were mountains on all sides, reflected everywhere in the narrow seas through which the boat glided. Now and then came houses and piers, funny little "baby" piers, at which the "Iona" stopped and took up or set down passengers, when every body rushed to the side to look on. Sunny rushed likewise; she became so interested and excited in watching the long waves the boat left behind her when her paddles began to move again, that her mamma was sometimes frightened out of her life that the child should overbalance herself, and tumble in. Once or twice poor mamma spoke so sharply that Sunny, utterly unaccustomed to this, turned round in mute surprise. But little girls, not old enough to understand danger, do not know what terrors mammas go through sometimes for their sakes.

It was rather a relief when Sunny became very hungry, and the bag of biscuits and the bottle of milk occupied her for a good while. Then she turned sleepy. The little Maymie's apron being secretly produced, she, laughing a little, began to suck it, under cover of mamma's shawl. Soon she went to sleep, and lay for nearly an hour in perfect peace, her eyes shut upon mountains, sea, and sky; and the sun shining softly upon her little face and her gold curls, that nestled close into mamma's shoulder. Such a happy child!

Almost cruel it seemed to wake her up, but necessary; for there came another change. The "Iona's" voyage was done. The next stage of the journey was through a canal, where were sights to be seen so curious that papa and mamma were as much interested in them as the little girl, who was growing quite an old traveller now. She woke up, rubbed her eyes, and, not crying at all, was carried ashore, and into the middle of another crowd. There was a deal of talking and scrambling, and rushing about with bags and cloaks, then all the heavier luggage was put into two gigantic wagons, which four great horses walked away with, and the passengers walked in a long string of twos and threes, each after the others, for about a quarter of a mile, till they came to the canal-side. There lay a boat so big, that it could only go forward and backward—I am sure if it had wanted to turn itself round it could not possibly have done so! On board of it all the people began to climb. Very funny people some of them were.

There was one big tall gentleman in a dress Sunny had never seen before—a cap on his head with a feather in it, a bag with furry tails dangling from his waist, and a petticoat like a little girl. He had also rather queer shoes and stockings, and when he took out from his ankle, as it seemed, a shiny-handled sort of knife, and slipped it back again, Sunny was very much surprised.

"Mamma," she whispered, "what does that gentleman keep his knife in his stocking for?" A question to which mamma could only answer "that she really didn't know. Perhaps he hadn't got a pocket."

"Sunny will give him her pocket — her French pinafore with pockets in it, shall she?"

Mamma thought the big Highlander might not care for Sunny's pretty muslin pinafore, with embroidery and Valenciennes lace, sewn for her by loving, dainty hands; and as the boat now moved away, and he was seen stalking majestically off along the road, there was no need to ask him the question. ·

For a little while the boat glided along the smooth canal, so close to either side that you felt as if you could almost pluck at the bushes, and ferns, and trailing brambles, with fast-ripening berries, that hung over the water. On the other side was a foot-road, where, a little way behind, a horse was dragging, with a long rope, a small, deeply-laden canal-boat, not pretty like this one, which went swiftly and merrily along by steam. But at last it came to a stand, in front of two huge wooden gates which shut the canal in, and through every crevice of which the pent-in water kept spouting in tiny cataracts.

"That's the first of the locks," said papa, who had seen it all before, and took his little girl to the end of the boat to show her the wonderful sight.

She was not old enough to have it explained or to understand what a fine piece of engineering work this canal is. It cuts across country from sea to sea, and the land not being level, but rising higher in the middle, and as you know water will not run up a hill-side and down again, these locks had to be made. They are, so to speak, boxes of water with double gates at either end. The boat is let into them, and shut in; then the water upon which it floats is gradually raised or lowered according as may be necessary, until it reaches the level of the canal beyond the second gate, which is opened and the boat goes in. There are eight or nine of these locks within a single mile—a very long mile, which occupies fully an hour. So the captain told his passengers they might get out and walk, which many of them did. But Sunshine, her papa and mamma, were much more amused in watching the great gates opening and shutting, and the boat rising or falling through the deep sides of the locks. Besides, the little girl called it "a bath," and expressed a strong desire to jump in and "swim like a fish," with mamma swimming after her! So mamma thought it as well to hold her fast by her clothes the whole time.

Especially when another interest came— three or four little Highland girls running alongside, jabbering gayly, and holding out glasses of milk. Her own bottle being nearly drained, Sunny begged for some; and the extraordinary difficulty papa had in stretching over to get the milk without spilling it, and return the empty glass without breaking it, was a piece of fun more delightful than even the refreshing draught. "Again!" she said, and wanted the performance all repeated for her private amusement.

She had now resumed her old tyranny over

her papa, whom she pursued everywhere. He could not find a single corner of the boat in which to hide and read his newspaper quietly, without hearing the cry, "Where's my papa? Sunny must go after papa," and there was the little figure clutching at his legs, "Take her up in your arms! up in your own arms!" To which the victim, not unwillingly, consented, and carried her everywhere.

Little Sunshine's next great diversion was dinner. It did not happen till late in the afternoon, when she had gone through, cheerfully as ever, another change of boat, and was steaming away through the open sea, which, however, was fortunately calm as a duck-pond, or what would have become of this little person?

Papa questioned very much whether she was not far too little a person to dine at the cabin-table with all the other grown-up passengers, but mamma answered for her that she would behave properly—she always did whenever she promised. For Sunny has the strongest sense of keeping a promise. Her one argument when wanting a thing, an argument she knows never denied, is, "Mamma, you promised." And her shoe-maker, who once neglected to send home her boots, has been im-

mortalized in her memory as "Mr. James So-
and-So, who broke his promise."

So, having promised to be good, she gravely
took her papa's hand and walked with him
down the long cabin to. her place at the table.
There she sat, quite quiet, and very proud of
her position. She ate little, being too deeply
occupied in observing every thing around her.
And she talked still less, only whispering mysteriously to her mamma once or twice,

"Sunny would like a potato, with butter on
it." "Might Sunny have one little biscuit—
just one?"

But she troubled nobody, spilt nothing, not
even her glass of water, though it was so big
that with both her fat hands she could scarcely
hold it; and said "Thank you" politely to a
gentleman who handed her a piece of bread.
In short, she did keep her promise, conducting
herself throughout the meal with perfect deco-
rum. But when it was over, I think she was
rather glad.

"Sunny may get down now?" she whispered; adding, "Sunny was quite good, she
was." For the little woman always likes to
have her virtues acknowledged.

And in re-mounting the companion-ladder,
rather a trial for her small legs, she looked at

the steward, who was taking his money, and observed to him in a confidential tone, "Sunny has had a good dinner; Sunny liked it"—at which the young man couldn't help laughing.

But every body laughs at Sunny, or with her—she has such an endless fund of enjoyment in every thing. The world to her is one perpetual kaleidoscope of ever-changing delights.

Immediately after dinner she had a pleasure quite new. Playing about the deck, she suddenly stopped and listened.

"Mamma, hark! there's music. May Sunny go after the music?" And her little feet began to dance rather than walk, as, pulling her mamma by the hand, she "went after" a German band that was playing at the other end of the vessel.

Little Sunshine had never before heard a band, and this was of wind instruments, played very well, as most German musicians can play. The music seemed to quiver all through her, down to her very toes. And when the dance-tune stopped, and her dancing feet likewise, and the band struck up the beautiful "Wacht am Rhein"—the Watch on the Rhine—(oh! if its singers had only stopped there, defending their fatherland, and not invaded the lands of other people!) this little girl, who knew nothing about French and Prussians, stood absorbed in solemn delight. Her hands were folded together (a trick she has), her face grew grave, and a soul far deeper than three years old looked out of her intent eyes. For when Sunny is earnest, she is *very* earnest; and when she turns furious, half a dozen tragedies seem written in her firm-set mouth, knitted brow, and flashing eyes.

She was disposed to be furious for a minute, when her Lizzie tried to get her away from the music. But her mamma let her stay, so she did stay close to the musicians, until the playing was all done.

It was growing late in the afternoon, near her usual bed-time, but no going to bed was possible. The steamboat kept ploughing on through lonely seas, dotted with many islands, larger or smaller, with high mountains on every side, some of them sloping down almost to the water's edge. Here and there was a solitary cottage or farm-house, but nothing like a town or village. The steamboat seemed to have the whole world to itself—sea, sky, mountains—a magnificent range of mountains! behind which the sun set in such splendor that papa and mamma, watching it together, quite forgot for

the time being the little person who was not
old enough to care for sunsets.

When they looked up, catching the sound of
her laughter, there she was, in a state of the
highest enjoyment, having made friends, all of
her own accord, with two gentlemen on board,
who played with her and petted her extremely. One of them had just taken out of his
pocket a wonderful bird, which jumped out of
a box, shook itself, warbled a most beautiful
tune, and then popped down in the box again;
not exactly a toy for a' child, as only about
half a dozen have ever been made, and they
generally cost about a hundred guineas apiece.

Of course Sunny was delighted. She listened intently to the warble, and whenever the
bird popped down and hid itself again, she gave
a scream of ecstasy. But she can not enjoy
things alone.

"May mamma come and see it? Mamma
would like to see it, she would!" And, running back, Sunny drew her mamma, with all
her little might, over to where the gentlemen
were sitting.

They were very polite to the unknown lady,
and went over the performance once again for
her benefit. And they were exceedingly kind
to her little girl, showing a patience quite won-

derful, unless, indeed, they had little girls of their own. They tried pertinaciously to find out Sunny's name, but she as persistently refused to disclose it—that is, any thing more than her Christian name, which is rather a peculiar one, and which she always gives with great dignity and accuracy, at full length. (Which, should they really have little girls of their own, and should they buy this book for them and read it, those two gentlemen will probably remember; nor think the worse of themselves that their kindness helped to while away what might otherwise have been rather dreary, the last hour of the voyage—a very long voyage for such a small traveller.)

It was ended at last. The appointed pier, a solitary place where only one other passenger was landed, stood out distinct in the last rays of sunset. Once again the child was carried across one of those shaky gangways—neither frightened nor cross, and quite cheerful and wide-awake still. Nay, she even stopped at the pier-head, her attention caught by some creatures more weary than herself.

Half a dozen forlorn sheep, their legs tied together, and their heads rolling about, with the most piteous expression in their open eyes, lay together, waiting to be put on board. The

G

child went up to them and stroked their
faces.

·   "Poor little baa-lambs, don't be so frightened; you won't be frightened, now Sunny has
patted you," said she, in her tenderest voice.
And then, after having walked a few yards,

"Sunny must go back.   Please, mamma,
may Sunny go back to say good-bye to those
poor little baa-lambs."

But the baa-lambs had already been tossed
on board, and the steamer was away with them
into the dark.   •

Into the dark poor little Sunny had also to
go; a drive of nine miles across country,
through dusky glens, and coming out by
loch sides, and under the shadow of great
mountains, above whose tops the stars were
shining.   Only the stars, for there was no
moon, and no lamps to the carriage; and the
driver, when spoken to, explained—in slow
Highland English, and in a mournful manner,
evidently not understanding the half of what
was said to him—that there were several miles
farther to go, and several hills to climb yet;
and that the horse was lame, and the road not
as safe as it might be.   A prospect which made
the elders of the party not perfectly happy, as
may well be imagined.

But the child was as merry as possible,
though it was long past her tea-time and she
had had no tea, and past bed-time, yet there
was no bed to go to; she kept on chattering
till it was quite dark, and then cuddled down,
making "a baby" of her mamma's hand—a
favorite amusement. And so she lay, the picture of peace, until the carriage stopped at the
welcome door, and there stood a friendly group
with two little boys in front of it. After
eleven hours of travelling, Little Sunshine had
reached a shelter at last!

CHAPTER VI.

SUNRISE among the mountains. Who that has ever seen it can forget it? Sunny's mamma never could. ·

Arriving here after dark, she knew no more of the place than the child did. But the first thing she did on waking next morning was to creep past the sofa where Sunny lay—oh, so fast asleep! having had a good scream overnight, as was natural after all her fatigues—steal cautiously to the window, and look out.

Such a sight! At the foot of a green slope, or sort of rough lawn, lay the little loch so often spoken of, upon which Sunny was to go a-fishing and catch big salmon with Maurice's papa. Round it was a ring of mountains, so high that they seemed to shut out half the sky. These were reflected in the water, so solidly and with such a sharp clear outline, that one could hardly believe it was only a reflection. Above their summit was one mass of deep rose-color, and this also was repeated in the loch, so that you could not tell which was reddest, the

water or the sky. Every thing was perfectly
still; not a ripple moved, not a leaf stirred, not
a bird was awake. An altogether new and
magic world.

Sunny was too much of a baby yet to care
for sunrise, or indeed for any thing just now,
except a good long sleep, so her mamma let her
sleep her fill; and when she woke at last, she
was as bright as a bird.

Long before she was dressed, she heard down
stairs the voices of the five little boys who
were to be her companions. Their papa and
mamma having no objection to their names
being told, I give them, for they were five very
pretty names: Maurice, Phil, Eddie, Franky,
and Austin Thomas. The latter being the
youngest, though by no means the smallest or
thinnest, generally had his name in full, with
variations, such as Austin Tummas, or Austin
Tummacks. Maurice, too, was occasionally called Maurie—but not often, being the eldest, you
see.

He was seven, very small for his age, but
with a face almost angelic in its delicate beauty. The first time Sunny saw him, a few
months before, she had seemed quite fasci-
nated by it, put her two hands on his shoulders,
and finally held up her mouth to kiss him—

which she seldom does to any children, rather preferring "grown-ups," as she calls them, for playfellows. She had talked ever since of Maurice, Maurice's papa, Maurice's boat, and especially of Maurice's "little baby," the only sister of the five boys. Yet when he came to greet her this morning, she was quite shy, and would not play with him or Eddie, or even Franky, who was nearer her own age; and when her mamma lifted up Austin Thomas, younger than herself, but much bigger in every way, and petted him a little, this poor little woman fell into great despair.

"Don't kiss him. I don't want you to kiss Austin Thomas!" she cried, and the passion which can rise at times in her merry blue eyes rose now. She clung to her mamma, almost sobbing.

Of course this was not right, and, as I said before, the little girl is not a perfect little girl. She is naughty at times, like all of us. Still, mamma was rather sorry for her. It was difficult for an only child, accustomed to have her mamma all to herself, to tumble suddenly into such a crowd of boys, and see that mamma could be kind to and fond of other children besides her own, as all mothers ought to be, without taking away one atom from the special mother's love, which no little people need be jealous over. Sunny bore the trial pretty well, on the whole. She did not actually cry —but she kept fast hold of her mamma's gown, and watched her with anxious eyes whenever she spoke to any other child, and especially to Austin Thomas.

The boys were very kind to her. Maurice went and took hold of her hand, trying to talk to her in his gentle way; his manners were as sweet as his face. Eddie, who was stronger and rougher, and more boyish, wanted her to go down with him to the pier—a small erection of stones at the shallow edge of the loch, where two or three boats always lay moored. Consequently the boys kept tumbling in and out of them, and in and out of the water too, very often—all day long. But the worst they ever could get was a good wetting—except Austin Thomas, who one day toddled in and slipped down, and, being very fat, could not pull himself up again; so that, shallow as the water was, he was very near being drowned. But Maurice and Eddie were almost "water babies"—so thoroughly at home in the loch —and Eddie, though under six years old, could already handle an oar.

"I can *low* " (row—he could not speak plain

yet). " I once lowed grandpapa all across the loch. Shall I low you and the little girl?"

But mamma rather hesitated at accepting the kind offer, and compromised the matter by going down to the pier with Sunny in her arms, to watch Eddie "low"—about three yards out and back again—in a carefully-moored boat. Sunny immediately wanted to go too, and mamma promised her she should, after breakfast, when papa was there to take care of her.

So the little party went back to the raised terrace in front of the house, where the sun was shining so bright, and where Phil, who was in delicate health, stood looking on with his pale, quiet face—sadly quiet and grave for such a child—and Franky, who was reserved and shy, stopped a moment in his solitary playing to notice the new-comer, but did not offer to go near her. Austin Thomas, however, kept pulling at her with his stout chubby arms, but whether he meant caressing or punching, it was difficult to say. Sunny opposed a dignified resistance, and would not look at Austin Thomas at all.

" Mamma, I want to stop with you. May Sunny stop with you?" implored she. " You said Sunny should go in the boat with you?"

Mamma always does what she says, if she possibly can, and besides, she felt a sympathy for her lonely child, who had not been much used to play with other children. So she kept Sunny beside her till they went down together —papa too—for their first row on the loch.

Such a splendid day! Warm but fresh—how could it help being fresh in that pure mountain air, which turned Sunny's cheeks the color of opening rose-buds, and made even papa and mamma feel almost as young as she? Big people like holidays as well as little people, and it was long since they had had a holiday. This was the very perfection of one, when every body did exactly as they liked: which consisted chiefly in doing nothing from morning till night.

Sunny was the only person who objected to idleness. She must always be doing something.

"I want to catch fishes," said she, after having sat quiet by mamma's side in the stern of the boat for about three minutes and a half: certainly not longer, though it was the first time she had ever been in a boat in all her life, and the novelty of her position sufficed to sober her for just that length of time. "I want to catch big salmon all by my own self."

A fishing-rod had, just as a matter of cere-
mony, been put into the boat; but as papa held
the two oars, and mamma the child, it was
handed over to Lizzie, who sat in the bow.
However, not a single trout offering to bite, it
was laid aside, and papa's walking-stick used
instead. This was shorter, more convenient,
and had a beautiful hooked handle which could
catch floating leaves. Leaves were much
more easily caught than fishes, and did quite
as well.

The little girl had now her heart's desire.
She was in a boat fishing.

"Sunny has caught a fish! Such a big
fish!" cried she in her shrillest treble of delight,
every time that event happened. And it happened so often that the bench was soon quite
"soppy" with wet leaves. Then she gave up
the rod, and fished with her hands, mamma
holding her as tight as possible, lest she should
overbalance, and be turned into a fish herself.
But water *will* wet; and mamma could not save
her from getting her poor little hands all blue
and cold, and her sleeves soaked through. She
did not like this; but what will not we endure,
even at two-and-three-quarters old, in pursuit
of some great ambition? It was not till her
hands were numbed, and her pinafore dripping,

that Sunny desisted from her fishing, and then only because her attention was caught by something else even more attractive.

" What's that, mamma? What's that?"

" Water-lilies."

Papa, busily engaged in watching his little girl, had let the boat drift upon a shoal of them, which covered one part of the loch like a floating island. They were so beautiful, with their leaves lying like green plates flat on the surface of the water, and their white flowers rising up here and there like ornamental cups. No wonder the child was delighted.

" Sunny wants a water-lily," said she, catching the word, though she had never heard it before. " May Sunny have one, two water-lilies? Two water-lilies! Please, mamma ?"

This was more easily promised than performed, for, in spite of papa's skill, the boat always managed to glide either too far off, or too close to, or right on the top of the prettiest flowers; and when snatched at, they always would dive down under water, causing the boat to lurch after them in a way particularly unpleasant. At last, out of about a dozen unsuccessful attempts, papa captured two expanded flowers, and one bud, all with long stalks. They were laid along the seat of the boat,

which had not capsized, nor had any body
tumbled out of it—a thing that mamma considered rather lucky, upon the whole, and insisted on rowing away out of the region of water-lilies.

"Let us go up the canal, then," said papa,
whom his host had already taken there, to
show him a very curious feature of the loch.

Leading out of one end of it, and communi-
cating between it and a stream that fed it from
the neighboring glen, was a channel, called
"the canal." Unlike most Highland streams,
it was as still as a canal; only it was natural,
not artificial. Its depth was so great, that a
stick fifteen feet long failed to find the bottom,
which, nevertheless, from the exceeding clear-
ness of the water, could be seen quite plain,
with the fishes swimming about, and the pebbles, stones, or roots of trees too heavy to float,
lying as they had lain, undisturbed, year after
year. The banks, instead of shallowing off,
went sheer down, as deep as in the middle, so
that you could paddle close under the trees
that fringed them—gnarled old oaks, queerly
twisted rowans or beeches, and nut-trees with
trunks so thick and branches so wide-spread-
ing, that the great-great-grandfathers of the glen
must have gone nutting there generations back..

• Yet this year they were as full as ever of nuts, the gathering of which frightened mamma nearly as much as the water-lilies. For papa, growing quite excited, *would* stand up in the boat and pluck at the branches, and would not. see that nutting on dry land, and nutting in a boat over fifteen or twenty feet of water, were two very different things. Even the little girl, imitating her elders, made wild snatches at the branches, and it was the greatest relief to mamma's mind when Sunny turned her attention to cracking her nuts, which her sharp little teeth did to perfection.

"Shall I give you one, mamma? Papa too?" And she administered them by turns out of her mouth, which if not the politest was the most convenient way. At last she began singing a song to herself, "Three little nuts all together! three little nuts all together!" Looking into the little girl's shut hands, mamma found—what she in all her long life had never found but once before, and that was many, many years ago—a triple nut—a "lucky" nut; as great a rarity as a four-leaved shamrock.

"Oh, what a prize! will Sunny give it to mamma?" (which she did immediately). "And mamma will put it carefully by, and keep it for Sunny till she is grown a big girl."

"Sunny is a big girl now; Sunny cracks nuts for papa and mamma."

Nevertheless, mamma kept the triple nut, as she remembered her own mamma keeping the former one, when she herself was a little girl. When Sunny grows a woman, she will find both.

Besides nuts, there were here and there along the canal-side long trailing brambles, with such huge blackberries on them—blackberries that seem to take a malicious pleasure in growing where nobody can get at them. Nobody could gather them except out of a boat, and then with difficulty. The best of them had after all to be left to the birds.

Oh, what a place this canal must have been for birds in spring! What safe nests might be built in these overhanging trees! what ceaseless songs sung there from morning till night! Now, being September, there were almost none. Dead silence brooded over the sunshiny crags and the motionless loch. When, far up among the hills, there was heard the crack of a gun—Maurice's papa's gun, for it could of course be no other—the sound, echoed several times over, was quite startling. What had been shot—a grouse, a snipe, a wild duck? Perhaps it was a roe deer? Papa was

all curiosity; but mamma, who dislikes shooting altogether, either of animals or men, and
can not endure the sight of a gun, even un-
loaded, was satisfied with hearing it at a distance, and counting its harmless echoes from
mountain to mountain.

What mountains they were!—standing in a
circle, gray, bare, silent, with their peaks far up
into the sky. Some had been climbed by the
gentlemen in this shooting lodge, or by Donald, the keeper, but it was hard work, and some
had never been climbed at all. The clouds
and mists floated over them, and sometimes,
perhaps, a stray grouse, or capercailzie, or
ptarmigan, paid them a visit, but that was all.
They were too steep and bare even for the roe
deer. Yet, oh! how grand they looked, grand
and calm, like great giants, whom nothing
small and earthly could affect at all.

The mountains were too big, as yet, for Little Sunshine. Her baby eyes did not take
them in. She saw them, of course, but she was
evidently much more interested in the nuts
overhead, and the fishes under water. And
when the boat reached "The Bower," she
thought it more amusing still.

"The Bower," so called, was a curious place,
where the canal grew so narrow, and the trees

so big, that the overarching boughs met in the middle, forming a natural arbor — only of water, not land—under which the boat swept for a good many yards. You had to stoop your head to avoid being caught by the branches, and the ferns and moss on either bank grew so close to your hand, that you could snatch at them as you swept by—which Little Sunshine thought the greatest fun in the world.

"Mamma, let me do it. Please, let Sunny do it her own self."

To do a thing "all my own self" is always a great attraction to this independent little person, and her mamma allows it whenever possible. Still there are some things which mammas may do, and little people may not, and this was one of them. It was obliged to be forbidden as dangerous, and Little Sunshine clouded over almost to tears. But she never worries her mamma for things, well aware that "No" means no, and "Yes," yes; and that neither are subject to alteration. And the boat being speedily rowed out of temptation's way into the open loch again, she soon found another amusement.

On the loch, besides waterfowl, such as wild ducks, teal, and the like, lived a colony of

geese. They had once been tame geese belonging to the farm, but they had emigrated, and
turned into wild geese, making their nests
wherever they liked, and bringing up their
families in freedom and seclusion. As to-
catching them like ordinary geese, it was hopeless; whenever wanted for the table they had
to be shot like game. This catastrophe had .
not happened lately, and they swam merrily
about—a flock of nine large white, lively, independent birds, which could be seen far off,
sailing about like a fleet of ships on the quiet
waters of the loch. They would allow you to
row within a reasonable distance of them, just
so close and no closer, then off they flew in a
body, with a great screeching and flapping of
wings—geese, even wild geese, being rather .
unwieldly birds.

Their chief haunt was a tiny island just at
the mouth of the canal, and there papa rowed,
just to have a look at them, for one was to
be shot for the Michaelmas dinner. (It never
was, by-the-bye, and, for all I know, still sails
cheerfully upon its native loch.)

"Oh, the ducks—the ducks!" (Sunny calls
all water-birds ducks.) She clapped her hands,
and away they flew, right over her head, at
once frightening and delighting her; then

H   .

watched them longingly until they dropped
down again, and settled in the farthest corner
of the loch.

"Might Sunny go after them? Might Sunny
·have a dear little duck to play with?"

The hopelessness of which desire might have
made her turn melancholy again, only just
then appeared, rowing with great energy, bris-
tling with fishing-rods, and crowded with little
people as well as "grown-ups," the big boat.
It was so busy that it hardly condescended to
notice the little pleasure-boat with only idle
people sailing about in the sunshine, and doing
nothing more useful than catching water-lilies
and frightening geese.

Still the little boat greeted the large one with
an impertinent hail of "Ship ahoy! what ship's
that?" and took in a cargo of small boys, who,
as it was past one o'clock, were wanted home
to the nursery dinner. And papa rowed the
whole lot of them back to the pier, where
every body was safely landed. Nobody tumbled in, and nobody was drowned — which
mamma thought, on the whole, was a great
deal to be thankful for.

CHAPTER .VII.

LIFE at the glen went on every day alike, in the simplest, happiest fashion, a sort of paradise of children, as in truth it was. Even the elders lived like children ; and big people and little people were together, more or less, all day long. A thing not at all objectionable when the children are good children, as these were.

The boys were noisy, of course, and, after the first hour of the morning, clean faces, hands, and clothes became a difficulty quite insurmountable, in which their mother had to resign herself to fate; as the mamma of five boys running about wild in the Highlands, necessarily must. But these were good, obedient, gentlemanly little fellows, and, had it been possible to keep them clean and whole, which it wasn't, very pretty little fellows too.

Of course they had a few boyish propensities, which increased the difficulty. Maurice, for instance, had an extraordinary love for all creeping things, and especially worms. On

the slightest pretense of getting bait to fish
with, he would go digging for them, and stuff
them into his pockets; whence, if you met him,
you were as likely as not to see one or two
crawling out. If you remonstrated he looked
unhappy, for Maurice really loved his worms.
He cherished them carefully, and did not in
the least mind their crawling over his hands,
his dress, or his plate. Only unfortunately
other people did. When scolded, he put his
pets meekly aside, but always returned to
them with the same love as ever. Perhaps
Maurice may turn out a great naturalist some
day.

The one idea of Eddie's life was boats. He
was forever at the little pier waiting a chance
of a row, and always wanting to "low" somebody, especially with "two oars," which he
handled uncommonly well for so small a child.
Fortunately for him, though not for his papa
and the salmon-fishers, the weather was dead
calm, so that it was like paddling on a duck-
pond; and the loch being shallow just at the
pier, except a few good wettings, which he
seemed to mind as little as if he were a frog,
bright, brave, adventurous Eddie came to no
harm.

Nor Franky, who imitated him admiringly

whenever he could. But Franky, who was
rather a reserved little man, and given to playing alone, had, besides the pier, another favorite
play-place, a hollow cut out in the rock to receive the burn which leaped down from the
hill-side just behind the house. Being close to
the kitchen door, it was put to all sorts of domestic uses, being generally full of pots and
pans, saucepans and kettles—not the most advisable playthings, but Franky found them
charming. He also unluckily found out something else—that the hollow basin had an out-
let, through which any substance, sent swimming down the swift stream, swam away beautifully for several yards, and then disappeared
underground. And the other end of this sub-
terraneous channel being in the loch, of course
it disappeared forever. In this way there vanished mysteriously all sorts of things—cups
and saucers, toys, pinafores, hats; which last
Franky was discovered in the act of making
away with, watching them floating off with extreme delight. It was no moral crime, and
hardly punishable, but highly inconvenient.
Sunny's beloved luggie, which had been carried about with her for weeks, was believed to
have disappeared in this way, and, as it could
not sink, is probably now drifting somewhere

about on the loch, to the great perplexity of
the fishes.

Ltitle Phil, alas! was too delicate to be mischievous. He crept about in the sunshine, not
playing with any body, but just looking on at
the rest, with his pale, sweet, pensive face. He
was very patient and good, and he suffered
very much. One day, hearing his uncle at
family prayers pray that God would make
him better, he sajd sadly, "If He does, I wish
He would make haste about it." Which was
the only complaint gentle pathetic little Phil
was ever heard to utter.

Sunny regarded him with some awe, as "the
poor little boy who was so ill." For herself, she
has never yet known what illness is; but she
is very sympathetic over it in others. Any
body's being "not well," will at once make
her tender and gentle; as she always was to
Phil. He in his turn was very kind to her;
lending her his "music," which was the greatest favor he could bestow or she receive.

This "music" was a box of infantile instruments, one for each boy—trumpet, drum, fife,
etc., making a complete band, which a rash-
minded but affectionate aunt had sent them,
and with which they marched about all day
long, to their own great delight and the cor-

responding despair of their elders. Phil, who had an ear, would go away quietly with his "music"—a trumpet, I think it was—and play it all by himself. But the others simply marched about in procession, each making the biggest noise he could, and watched by Sunny with admiration and envy. Now and then, out of great benevolence, one of the boys would lend her his instrument, and nobody did this so often as Phil, though of them all he liked playing his music the best. The picture of him sitting on the door-step, with his pale fingers wandering over his instrument, and his sickly face looking almost contented as he listened to the sound, will long remain in every body's mind. Sunny never objected to her mamma's carrying him, as he often had to be carried; though he was fully six years old. He was scarcely heavier than the little girl herself. Austin Thomas would have made two of him.

Austin's chief peculiarity was this amiable fatness. He tumbled about like a roly-poly pudding, amusing every body, and offending no one but Little Sunshine. But his persistent pursuit of her mamma, whom he insisted on calling "Danmamma" (grandmamma), and following whenever he saw her, was more than

the little girl could bear, and she used to knit
her brows and look displeased. However,
mamma never took any notice, knowing what
a misery to itself and all about it is a jealous
child.

Amidst these various amusements passed
the day. It began at 8 A.M., when Sunshine
and her mamma usually appeared on the terrace in front of the house. They two were
" early birds," and so they got " the worm"—
that is, a charming preliminary breakfast of
milk, bread and butter, and an egg, which they
usually ate on the door-step. Sometimes the
rest, who had had their porridge, the usual
breakfast of Scotch children—and very nice
it is, too—gathered round for a share ; which
it was pleasant to give them, for they waited
so quietly, and were never rough or rude.

Nevertheless, sometimes difficulties arose.
The tray being placed on the gravel, Maurice
often sat beside it, and his worms would crawl
out of his pocket and on to the bread and
butter. Then Eddie now and then spilt the
milk, and Austin Thomas would fill the salt-
cellar with sand out of the gravel-walk, and
stir it all up together with the egg-spoon ; a
piece of untidiness which Little Sunshine re-
sented extremely.

She had never grown reconciled to Austin Thomas. In spite of his burly good-nature, and his broad beaming countenance (which earned him the nickname of " Cheshire," from his supposed likeness to the Cheshire Cat in "Alice's Adventures"), she refused to play with him; whenever he appeared, her eye followed him with distrust and suspicion, and when he said " Danmamma," she would contradict him indignantly.

" It isn't grandmamma, it's *my* mamma, my own mamma. Go away, naughty boy !" If he presumed to touch the said mamma, it was always, "Take me up in your arms, in your own arms "—so as to prevent all possibility of Austin Thomas's getting there.

But one unlucky day Austin tumbled down, and, though more frightened than hurt, cried so much that, his own mamma being away, Sunny's mamma took him and comforted him, soothing him on her shoulder till he ceased sobbing. This was more than human nature could bear. Sunny did nothing at the time, except pull frantically at her mamma's gown, but shortly afterwards she and Austin Thomas were found by themselves, engaged in single combat on the gravel. walk. She had seized him by the collar of his frock, and was kicking

him with all her might, while he on his part
was pommelling at her with both his little fat
fists, like an infant prize-fighter. It was a
pitched battle, pretty equal on both sides; and
conducted so silently, in such dead earnest,
that it would have been quite funny—if it had
not been so very wrong.

Of course, such things could not be allowed,
even in babies under three years old. Sunny's
mamma ran to the spot and separated the com-
batants by carrying off her own child right
away into the house. Sunny was so astonished
that she did not say a word. And when she
found that her mamma never said a word neither, but bore her along in total silence, she
was still more surprised. Her bewilderment
was at its height, when, shutting the bed-room
door, her mamma set her down, and gave
her—not a whipping: she objects to whipping under any circumstances—but the se-
verest scolding the child had ever had in her
life.

When I say "scolding," I mean a grave sor-
rowful rebuke, showing how wicked it was to
kick any body, and how it grieved mamma
that her good little girl should be so exceedingly naughty. Mamma grieved is a reproach
under which Little Sunny breaks down at

once. Her lips began to quiver; she hung her head sorrowfully.

"Sunny had better go into the cupboard," suggested she.

"Yes, indeed," mamma replied. "I think the cupboard is the only place for such a naughty little girl; go in at once."

So poor Sunshine crept solemnly into a large press with sliding doors, used for hanging up clothes, and there remained in silence and darkness all the while her mamma was dressing to go out. At last she put her head through the opening.

"Sunny quite good now, mamma."

"Very well," said mamma, keeping with difficulty a grave countenance. "But will Sunny promise never to kick Austin Thomas again?"

"Yes."

"Then she may come out of the cupboard and kiss mamma."

Which she did, with a beaming face, as if nothing at all had happened. But she did not forget her naughtiness. Some days after, she came up, and confidentially informed her mamma, as if it were an act of great virtue, "Mamma, Sunny 'membered her promise. Sunny hasn't kicked the little boy again."

After the eight o'clock breakfast, Sunny, her mamma, and the five little boys, generally took a walk together, or sat telling stories in front of the house, till the ten o'clock breakfast of the elders. That over, the party dispersed their several ways, wandering about by land or water, and meeting occasionally, great folks and small, in boats, or by hill-sides, or in-doors at the children's one o'clock dinner — almost the only time, till night, that any body ever was in-doors.

Besides most beautiful walks for the elders, there were, close by the house, endless play-places for the children, each more attractive than the other. The pier. on the loch was the great delight; but there was about a hundred yards from the house a burn (in fact, burns were always tumbling from the hill-side, wherever you went), with a tiny bridge across it, which was a charming spot for little people. There usually assembled a whole parliament of ducks, and hens, and chickens, quacking and clucking and gobbling together; to their own great content and that of the children, especially the younger ones. Thither came Austin Thomas with his nurse Grissel, a thorough Scotch lassie; and Sunny with her English Lizzie; and there the baby, the pet of all, tiny

"Miss Mary," a soft dainty cuddling thing of six months old, used to be brought to lie and sleep in the sunshine, watched by Little Sunshine with never-ending interest. She would go anywhere with "the dear little baby." The very intonation of her voice, and the expression of her eyes, changed as she looked at it— for this little girl is passionately fond of babies.

Farther down the mountain-road was another attractive corner, a stone dike, covered with innumerable blackberries. Though gathered daily, there were each morning more to gather, and they furnished an endless feast for both nurses and children. And really in this sharp mountain air, the hungriness of both big and little people must have been alarming. How the house-mother ever fed her household, with the only butcher's shop ten miles off, was miraculous. For very often the usual resort of shooting-lodges entirely failed: the game was scarce, and hardly worth shooting, and in this weather the salmon absolutely refused to be caught. Now and then a mournful-looking sheep was led up to the door, and offered for sale alive, to be consumed gradually as mutton. But when you have to eat an animal right through, you generally get a little tired of him at last.

The food that never failed, and nobody ever
wearied of, was the trout; large dishes of
which appeared, and disappeared, every morning at breakfast. A patient guest, who could
not go shooting, used to sit fishing for trout,
hour by hour, in the cheerfullest manner;
thankful for small blessings (of a pound or
a pound and a half at most), and always hoping for the big salmon which he had travelled
three hundred miles to fish for, but which
never came. Each day, poor gentleman! he
watched the dazzlingly bright sky, and catching
the merest shadow of a cloud, would say cour-
ageously, "It looks like rain! Perhaps the
salmon may bite to-morrow."

Of afternoons, Sunny and her mamma generally got a little walk and talk alone together
along the hill-side road, noticing every thing,
and especially the Highland cattle, who went
about in family parties—the big bull, a splendid animal, black or tawny, looking very fierce,
but really offering no harm to any body; half
a dozen cows, and about twice that number of
calves. Such funny little things these were!
not smooth, like English calves, but with quan-
tities of shaggy hair hanging about them, and
especially over their eyes. Papa used to say
that his little girl, with her incessant activi-

ty, and her yellow curls tossing wildly about on her forehead, was very like a Highland calf.

At first, Sunny was rather afraid of these extraordinary beasts, so different from Southern cattle; but she soon got used to them, and as even the big bull did nothing worse than look at her, and pass her by, she would stand and watch them feeding with great interest, and go as close to them as ever she was allowed. Once she even begged for a little calf to play with, but as it ran away up the mountain-side as active as a deer, this was not practicable. And on the whole she liked the ducks and chickens best.

And for a change she liked to walk with mamma round the old-fashioned garden. What a beautiful garden it was!—shut in with high walls, and sloping southward down to the loch. No doubt many a Highland dame, generations back, had taken great pleasure in it, for its fruit-trees were centuries old, and the box edging of its straight smooth gravel walks was a picture in itself. Also a fuchsia hedge, thick with crimson blossoms, which this little girl, who is passionately fond of flowers, could never pass without begging for "a posie, to stick in my little bosie," where it was kissed and "loved" until, generally soon enough! it got broken and died.

Equally difficult was it to pass the apples which lay strewn about under the long lines of espaliers, where Maurice and Eddie were often seen hovering about with an apple in each hand, and plenty more in each pocket. The Highland air seemed to give them unlimited digestion, but Sunny's mamma had occasionally to say to her little girl that quiet denial, which caused a minute's sobbing, and then, known to be inevitable, was submitted to.

The child found it hard sometimes that little girls might not do all that little boys may. For instance, between the terrace and the pier was a wooden staircase with a hand-rail; both rather old and rickety. About this hand-rail the boys were forever playing, climbing up it and sliding down it. Sunny wanted to do the same, and one day her mamma caught her perched astride at the top, and preparing to "slidder" down to the bottom, in imitation of Eddie, who was urging her on with all his might. This most dangerous proceeding for little girls with frocks had to be stopped at once; mamma explaining the reason, and insisting that Sunny must promise never to do it again. Poor little woman, she was very sad; but she did promise, and moreover she kept her word. Several times mamma saw her stand watching the boys with a mournful countenance, but she never got astride on the hand-rail again. Only once—a sudden consolation occurred to her.

" Mamma, 'posing Sunny were some day to grow into a little boy, *then* she might slide down the ladder?"

"Certainly, yes!" answered mamma with great gravity, and equal sincerity. In the mean time she perfectly trusted her reliable child, who never does any thing behind her back any more than before her face. And she let her clamber about as much as was practicable, up and down rocks, and over stone dikes, and in and out of burns, since, within certain limitations, little girls should be as active as little boys. And by degrees, Sunny, a strong, healthy, energetic child, began to follow the boys about everywhere.

There was a byre and a hay-house, where the children were very fond of playing, climbing up a ladder and crawling along the roof to the ridge-tiles, along which Eddie would drag himself astraddle from end to end, throwing Sunny into an ecstasy of admiration. To climb

I

up to the top of a short ladder and be held there, whence she could watch Eddie crawl like a cat from end to end of the byre, and wait till he slided down the tiles again, was a felicity for which she would even sacrifice the company of "the dear little baby."

But after all, the pier was the great resort. From early morning till dark, two or three of the children were always to be seen there, paddling in the shallows like ducks, with or without shoes and stockings, assisting at every embarkation or landing of the elders, and generally, by force of entreaties, getting — Eddie especially—"a low" on their own account several times a day. Even Sunny gradually came to find such fascination in the water, and in Eddie's company, that if her mamma had not kept a sharp look-out after her, and given strict orders that, without herself, Sunny was never under any pretext to go on the loch at all, the two children, both utterly fearless, would certainly have been discovered sailing away like the wise men of Gotham who "went to sea in a bowl." Probably with the same ending to their career; that—

> "If the bowl had been stronger,
> My song would have been longer!"

After Little Sunshine's holiday was done, mamma, thinking over the countless risks run, by her own child and these other children, felt thankful that they had all left this beautiful glen alive.

CHAPTER VIII.

THE days sped so fast with these happy people, children and "grown-ups," as Sunny calls them, that soon it was already Sunday, the first of the only two Sundays they had to spend at the glen. Shall I tell about them both?

These parents considered Sunday the best day in all the week, and tried to make it so; especially to the children, whom, in order to give the servants rest, they then took principally into their own hands. They wished, that when the little folks grew up, Sunday should always be remembered as a bright day, a cheerful day, a day spent with papa and mamma; when nobody had any work to do, and every body was merry, and happy, and good. Also clean, which was a novelty here. Even the elders rather enjoyed putting on their best clothes with the certainty of not getting them wetted in fishing-boats, or torn with briers and brambles on hill-sides. Church was not till twelve at noon, so most of the party went a leisurely morning stroll, and Sunny's·papa and mamma decided to have a quiet row on the loch, in a clean boat, all by their two selves. But, as it happened, their little girl, taking a walk with her Lizzie, espied them afar off.

Faintly across the water came the pitiful entreaty, "Papa! mamma! Take her. Take her with you." And the little figure, running as fast as her fat legs would carry her, was seen making its way, with Lizzie running after, to the very edge of the loch.

What heart would not have relented? Papa rowed back as fast as he could, and took her in, her face quivering with delight, though the big tears were still rolling down her cheeks. But April showers do not dry up faster than Sunny's tears.

No fishing to-day, of course. Peacefully they floated down the loch, which seemed to know it was Sunday, and to lie, with the hills standing round it, more restful, more sunshiny, more beautiful than ever. Not a creature was stirring; even the cattle that always clustered on a little knoll above the canal, made motion-less pictures of themselves against the sky, as if they were sitting or standing for their portraits, and would not move upon any account. Now and then, as the boat passed, a bird in the bushes fluttered, but not very far off, and then sat on a bough and looked at it, too fearless of harm to fly away. Every thing was so intensely still, so unspeakably beautiful, that when mamma, sitting in the stern, with her arm fast round her child, began to sing "Jerusalem the Golden," and afterwards that other beautiful hymn, "There is a land of pure delight," the scene around appeared like an earthly picture of that Celestial Land.

They rowed homeward just in time to dress for church, and start, leaving the little girl behind. She was to follow by-and-by with her Lizzie, and be taken charge of by mamma while Lizzie went to the English service in the afternoon.

This was the morning service, and in Gaelic. With an English prayer-book it was just possible to follow it and guess at it, though the words were unintelligible. But they sounded very sweet, and so did the hymns; and the small congregation listened as gravely and reverently as if it had been the grandest church in the world, instead of a tiny room, no bigger than an ordinary sitting-room, with a communion-table of plain deal, and a few rows of deal benches, enough to seat about twenty people, there being about fifteen present to-day. Some of them had walked several miles, as they did every Sunday, and often, their good clergyman said, when the glen was knee-deep in snow.

He himself spent his quiet days among them, winter and summer, living at a farm-house near, and scarcely ever quitting his charge. A lonelier life, especially in winter-time, it was hardly possible to imagine. Yet he looked quite contented, and so did the little congregation, as they listened to the short Gaelic sermon (which, of course, was incomprehensible to the strangers), then slowly went out of church and stood hanging about on the dike-side in the sunshine, till the second service should begin.

Very soon, a few more groups were seen advancing towards church. There was Maurice, prayer-book in hand, looking so good and gentle and sweet, almost like a cherub in a picture; and Eddie, not at all cherubic, but entirely boyish, walking sedately beside his papa; Eddie clean and tidy, as if he had never torn his clothes or dirtied his face in all his life. Then came the children's parents, papa and mamma and their guests, and the servants of the house following. While far behind, holding cautiously by her Lizzie's hand, and rather alarmed at her new position, was a certain little person, who, as soon as she saw her own papa and

mamma, rushed frantically forward to meet
them with a cry of irrepressible joy.

"Sunny wants to go to church! Sunny
would like to go to church with the little boys,
and Lizzie says she mustn't."

Lizzie was quite right, mamma explained;
afraid that so small a child might only inter-
rupt the worship, which she could not possibly
understand. But she compromised the matter
by promising that Sunny should go to church
as soon as ever she was old enough, and to-day
she should stay with mamma, out in the sunshiny road, and hear the singing from outside.

Staying with mamma being always sufficient
felicity, she consented to part with the little
boys, and they passed on into church.

By this time the post, which always came in
between the services on Sundays, appeared, and
the post-master, who was also school-master and
beadle at the church—as the school, the church,
and the post-office, were all one building—began arranging and distributing the contents of
the bag.

Every body sat down by the roadside and
read their letters. Those who had no letters
opened the newspapers—those cruel newspapers, full of the war. It was dreadful to read
them, in this lovely spot, on this calm Septem-

ber Sunday, with the good pastor and his innocent flock preparing to begin the worship of
Him who commanded "Love your enemies;
bless them that curse you, do good to them
that hate you, and pray for them that despite-
fully use you and persecute you."

Oh, what a mockery "church" seemed! You
little children can·never understand the pain
of it; but you will when you are grown up.
May God grant that in your time you may
never suffer as we have done, but. that His
mercy may then have brought permanent
peace; beating "swords into ploughshares, and
spears into pruning-hooks," for ever and ever,
throughout the world!

Sunny's mamma prayed so with all her heart,
when, the newspaper laid down, she sat on a
stone outside the church, with her child playing beside her; far enough not to disturb the
congregation, but near enough to catch a good
deal of the service, which was the English
Episcopal service; there being few Presbyteri-
ans in this district of Scotland, and not a Pres-
byterian church within several miles.

Presently a harmonium began to sound, and
a small choir of voices, singing not badly, began
the *Magnificat.* It was the first time in her life
that the little girl had heard choral music—sev-

eral people singing all together. She pricked up her ears at once, with the expression of intense delight that all kinds of music bring into her little face.

"Mamma, is that church? Is that my papa singing?"

Mamma did not think it was, but it might be Maurice's papa, and his mamma, and Lizzie, and several other people; Sunny must listen and be quite quiet, so as not to disturb them.

So she did, good little girl! sitting as mute as a mouse all the while the music lasted, and when it ceased, playing about, still quietly; building pebble mountains, and gathering a few withered leaves to stick on the top of them. For she and her mamma were sitting on the gravel walk of the school-master's garden; beside a row of flower-pots, still radiant with geraniums and fuchsias. They were so close to the open window under which stood the pulpit, that mamma was able to hear almost every word of the sermon—and a very good sermon it was.

When it ended, the friendly little congregation shook hands and talked a little; then separated, half going up and the other half down the road. The minister came home to dinner, walking between Maurice and Eddie, of whom

he was a particular friend. They always looked forward to this weekly visit of his as one of
the Sunday enjoyments, for he was an admirable hand at an oar, and Eddie, who tyrannized
over him in the most affectionate way, was
quite sure of " a low " when the minister was
there.

So, after dinner, all went out together, parents and children, pastor and flock, in two
boats, and rowed peacefully up and down the
loch, which had fallen into the cool gray shadow of evening, with the most gorgeous sunset-
light resting on the mountains opposite, and
gradually fading away, higher and higher, till
the topmost peaks alone kept the glow. But
that they did to the very last; like a good man
who, living continually in the smile of God,
lives cheerfully on to the end.

Sunny and her mamma watched the others,
but did not go out, it being near the child's
bedtime; and unless it is quite unavoidable,
nobody ever puts Sunny to bed, or hears her
say her little prayers, except her own mamma.
She went to sleep quite happily, having now
almost forgotten to ask for Tommy Tinker, or
any other story. The continual excitement of
her life here left her so sleepy that the minute
she had her little night-gown on, she was ready

to shut her eyes and go off into what mamma calls "the land of Nod."

And so ended, for her, the first Sunday in the glen, which, in its cheerful, holy peace, was a day long to be remembered. But the little boys, Maurice and Eddie, who did not go to bed so early, after the loch grew dark, and the rowing was all done, spent a good long evening in the drawing-room, climbing on the minister's knees, and talking to him about boats and salmon, and all sorts of curious things : he was so very kind to little children. And after the boys were gone to bed, he and the elder folk gathered round the not unwelcome fire, and talked too. This good minister, who spent his life in the lonely glen, with very little money—so little that rich Southern people would hardly believe an educated clergyman could live upon it at all—and almost no society, except that of the few cottagers and farmers scattered thinly up and down, yet kept his heart up, and was cheerful and kindly, ready to help old and young, rich and poor, and never complaining of his dull life, or any thing else—this gentleman, I say, was a pattern to both great folk and small.

The one only subject of discontent in the house, if any body could feel discontent in such

a pleasant place and amid such happy circumstances, was the continued fine weather. While
the sky remained unclouded, and the loch as
smooth as glass, no salmon would bite. They
kept jumping up in the liveliest and most pro-
voking way; sometimes you could see their
heads and shoulders clean out of water, and
of course they looked bigger than any salmon
ever seen before. Vainly did the master of
the house and his guests go after them whenever there was the least cloud on the sky, and
coax them to bite with the most fascinating
flies and most alluring hooks: they refused to
take the slightest notice of either. Only trout,
and they not big ones, ever allowed themselves
to be caught.

The children and mammas, delighting in the
warm sunshiny weather, did not grieve much,
but the gentlemen became quite low in their
spirits, and at last, for their sakes, and especially for the sake of that one who only cared for
fishing, and had come so far to fish, the whole
household began to watch the sky, and with
great self-sacrifice to long for a day—a whole
day—of good, settled, pelting rain.

And on the Monday following this bright
Sunday, it seemed likely. The morning was
rather dull, the sunshiny haze which hung over

the mountains melted away, and they stood
out sharp and dark and clear.- Towards noon,
the sky clouded over a little—a very little!
Hopefully the elders sat down to their four
o'clock dinner, and by the time it was over a
joyful cry arose, .

" It's raining ! it's raining !"

Every body started up in the greatest delight. "Now we.shall have a chance of a salmon !" cried the gentlemen, afraid to hope too
much. Nevertheless, they hastily put on their
great-coats, and rushed down to the pier, armed
with a rod apiece, and with Donald the keeper to row them; because if they did hook a
salmon, Eddie explained, they would want
somebody to "low" the boat, and follow the
fish wherever he went. Eddie looked very
unhappy that he himself had not this duty, of
which he evidently thought he was capable.
But when his father told him he could not go,
he obeyed, as he always did. He was very
fond of his father.

The three boys, Maurice, Eddie, and Franky
—Phil, alas ! was too ill to be much excited,
even over salmon-fishing—resigned themselves
to fate, and made the best of things by climbing on the drawing-room table, which stood in
front of the window, and thence watching the

SUNNY'S MAMMA TELLING STORIES.

boat as it moved slowly up and down the gray loch, with the four motionless figures sitting in it—sitting contentedly soaking. The little boys, Eddie especially, would willingly have sat and soaked too, if allowed.

At length, as some slight consolation, and to prevent Eddie's dangling his legs out at the open window, letting in the wind and the rain, and running imminent risk of tumbling out, twenty feet or so, down to the terrace below, Sunny's mamma brought a book of German pictures, and proposed telling stories out of them.

They were very funny pictures, and have been Little Sunshine's delight for many months. So she, as the owner, displayed them proudly to the rest, and it having been arranged with some difficulty how six pairs of eyes could look over the same book, the party arranged themselves thus: Sunny's mamma sat on the hearth-rug, with her own child on her lap, Austin Thomas on one side, and Phil on the other; while Maurice, Eddie, and Franky managed as well as they could to look over her shoulders. There was a general sense of smothering and huddling up, like a sparrow's nest when the young ones are growing a little too big: but every body appeared

K

happy. Now and then, Sunshine knitted her brows fiercely, as she can knit them on occasion, when Austin Thomas came crawling too close upon her mamma's lap, with his intrusively affectionate " Danmamma," but no open quarrel broke out. The room was so cosy and bright with fire-light, and every body was so comfortable, that they had almost forgotten the rain outside, also the salmon-fishing, when . the door suddenly opened, and in burst the cook.

Mary was a kind, warm-hearted Highland woman, always ready to do any thing for any body, and particularly devoted to the children. Gaelic was easier to her than English always, but now she was so excited that she could hardly get out her words.

" Master's hooked a salmon ! He's been crying" (calling) "on Neil to get out another boat and come to him. It must be a very big salmon, for he is playing him up and down the loch. They've been at it these ten minutes and more.

Mary's excitement affected the mistress, who laid down her baby. " Where are they? Has any body seen them?"

" Any body, ma'am ? Why every body's down at the shore looking at them. The minister too ; he was passing, and stopped to see."

As a matter of course, cook evidently thought. Even a minister could not pass by such an interesting sight. Nor did she seem in the least surprised when the mistress sent for her water-proof cloak, and, drawing the hood over her head, went deliberately out into the pelting rain, Maurice and Franky following. As for Eddie, at the first mention of salmon, he had been off like a shot, and was now seen standing on the very edge of the pier, gesticulating with all his might for somebody to take him into a boat. Alas! in vain.

Never was there such an all-absorbing salmon. As Mary had said, the whole household was out watching him and his proceedings. The baby, Austin Thomas, Sunny, and Sunny's mamma, were left alone, to take care of one another.

These settled down again in front of the fire, and Sunny, who had been a little bewildered by the confusion, recovered herself, and, not at all alive to the importance of salmonfishing, resumed her entreating whisper.

"'Bout German pictures, mamma; tell me 'bout German pictures."

And she seemed quite glad to go back to

her old ways; for this little girl likes nothing better than snuggling into her mamma's lap, on the hearth rug, and being told about German pictures.

They came to her all the way from Germany as a present from a kind German friend, and some of them are very funny. They make regular stories, a story on each page. One is about a little greedy boy, so like a pig, that at last being caught with a sweetmeat by.an old witch, she turns him into a pig in reality. He is put into a sty, and just about to be killed, when his sister comes in to save him with a fairy rose in her hand; the witch falls back, stuck through with her own carving-knife, and poor piggy-wiggy, touched by the magic rose, turns into a little boy again. Then there is another page, "'bout èffelants," as Sunny calls them—a papa elephant and a baby elephant taking a walk together. They come across the first Indian railway, and the papa elephant, who has never seen a telegraph wire before, is very angry at it and pulls it down with his trunk. Then there comes whizzing past a railway-train, which makes him still more indignant, as he does not understand it at all. He talks very seriously on the subject to his little son, who listens with a respectful air. Then, determined to put an end to such nuisances, this wise papa elephant marches right in front of the next train that passes. He does not stop it, of course, but it stops him, cutting him up into little pieces, and throwing him on either side the line. At which the little elephant is so frightened that you see him taking to his heels, very solid heels too, and running right away.

Sunny heard this story for the hundredth time, delighted as ever, and then tried to point out to Austin Thomas which was the papa "effelant" and which the baby "effelant." But Austin Thomas's more infantile capacity did not take it in; he only "scrumpled" the pages with his fat hands, and laughed. There might soon have been an open war if mamma had not soothed her little girl's wounded feelings by the great felicity of taking off her shoes and stockings, and letting her warm her little feet by the fire, while she lay back on her mamma's lap, sucking her Maymie's apron.

The whole group were in this state of perfect peace: outside it had grown dark, and mamma had stirred the fire and promised to begin a quite new story, when the door again opened and Eddie rushed in. Maurice and Frankie followed, wet, of course, to the skin—

for each left a little pool of water behind him
wherever he stood—but speechless with excitement. Shortly after, up came the three
gentlemen, likewise silent, but not from excitement at all.

"But where's the salmon?" asked Sunny's
mamma. "Pray let us see the salmon."

Maurice's papa looked as solemn as—what
shall I say? the renowned Buff, when he—

> "Strokes his face with a sorrowful grace,
> And delivers his staff to the next place."

He delivered his—no, it was not a stick but
a "tommy" hat, all ornamented with fishing-
flies, and dripping with rain, to any body that
would hang it up, and sank into a chair, saying
mournfully,

"You can't see the salmon."

"Why not?"

"Because he's at the bottom of the loch.
He got away."

"Got away!"

"Yes, after giving us a run of a full hour."

"An hour and five minutes by my watch,"
added Sunny's papa, who looked as dejected
as the other two. Though no salmon-fisher,
he had been so excited by the sport that he
had sat drenched through and through, in the

stern of the boat, and afterwards declared "he didn't know it had rained."

"Such a splendid fish he was—twenty-five pounds at least."

"Twenty," suggested some one, who was put down at once with scorn.

"Twenty-five, I am certain, for he rose several times, and I saw him plain. So did Donald. Oh, what a fish he was! And he bit upon a trout-line! To think that we should have had that one trout-line with us, and he chose it. It could hardly hold him, of course. He required the tenderest management. We gave him every chance" (of being killed, poor fish!) "The minute he was hooked, I threw the oars to Donald, who pulled beautifully, humoring him up and down, and you should have seen the dashes he made! He was so strong—such a big fish!"

"Such a big fish!" echoed Eddie, who stood listening with open mouth and eyes that gradually become as melancholy as his father's.

"And, as I said, we played him for an hour and five minutes. He was getting quite exhausted, and I had just called to Neil to row close and put the gaff under him, when he came up to the surface—I declare, just as if he wanted to have a stare at me—then made a sudden dart, right under the boat. No line could stand that, a trout-line especially."

"So he got away?"

"Of course he did, with my hook in his mouth, the villain! I dare say he has it there still."

It did occur to Sunny's mamma that the fish was fully as uncomfortable as the fisherman, but she durst not suggest this for the world. Evidently, the salmon had conducted himself in a most unwarrantable manner, and was worthy of universal condemnation.

Even after the confusion had a little abated, and the younger children were safely in bed, twenty times during tea he was referred to in the most dejected manner, and his present position angrily speculated upon—whether he would keep the hook in his mouth for the remainder of his natural life, or succeed in rubbing it off among the weeds at the bottom of the loch.

" To be sure he will, and be just as cheerful as ever, the wretch! Oh that I had him—hook and all! For it was one of my very best flies."

" Papa, if you would let me ' low ' you in the boat, while you fished, perhaps he might come and bite again to-morrow?"

This deep diplomatic suggestion of Eddie's

did not meet with half the success it deserved. Nobody noticed it except his mother, and she only smiled.

"Well!" she said, trying to cheer up the mournful company. "Misfortunes can't be helped sometimes. It is sad. Twenty-five pounds of fish; boiled, fried into steaks, kippered. Oh dear! what a help in the feeding of the household!"

"Yes," said the patient gentleman, who, being unable to walk, could only sit and fish, and, having come all the way from London to catch a salmon, had never yet had a bite except this one. "Yes, twenty-five pounds at two shillings the pound—Billingsgate price now. That makes two-pound-ten of good English money gone to the bottom of the loch!"

Every body laughed at this practical way of putting the matter, and the laugh a little raised the spirits of the gentlemen. Though still they mourned, and mourned, looking as wretched as if they had lost their whole families in the loch, instead of that unfortunate—or fortunate—salmon.

"It isn't myself I care for," lamented Maurice's papa. "It's you others. For I know you will have no other chance. The rain will clear off—it's clearing off now, into a beautiful starlight night. To-morrow will be another of those dreadfully sunshiny days. Not a fish will bite, and you will have to go home at the week's end—and there's that salmon lying snugly in his hole, with my hook in his mouth!"

"Never mind," said the patient gentleman, who, though really the most to be pitied, bore his disappointment better than any body. "There's plenty of fish in the loch, for I've seen them every day jumping up ; and somebody will catch them, if I don't. After all, we had an hour's good sport with that fellow to-day—and it was all the better for him that he got away."

With which noble sentiment the good man took one of the boys on his knee—his godson, for whom he was planning an alliance with his daughter, a young lady of four-and-a-half, and began discussing the settlements he expected—namely, a large cake on her side, and on the young gentleman's, at least ten salmon out of the loch, to be sent in a basket to London. With this he entertained both children and parents, so that every body grew merry as usual, and the lost salmon fell into the category of misfortunes over which the best dirge is the shrewd Scotch proverb, "It's nae use greeting ower spilt milk."

CHAPTER IX.

THE forebodings of the disappointed salmon-fishers turned out true. That wet
Monday was the first and last day of rain, for
weeks. Scarcely ever had such a dry season
been known in the glen. Morning after morning the gentlemen rowed out in a hopeless
manner, taking their rods with them, under a
sky cloudless and hot as June: evening after
evening, if the slightest ripple arose, they went
out again, and floated about lazily in the gorgeous sunset, but not a salmon would bite.
Fish after fish, each apparently bigger than
the other, kept jumping up, sometimes quite
close to the boat. Some must have swum under the line and looked at it, made an exami-
nation of the fly and laughed at it, but as for
swallowing it, Oh dear, no! Not upon any account.

What was most tantalizing, the gardener,
going out one day, without orders, and with
one of his master's best lines, declared he had

hooked a splendid salmon! As it got away, and also carried off the fly, a valuable one, perhaps it was advisable to call it a salmon, but nobody quite believed this. It might have been only a large trout.

By degrees, as salmon-fishing, never plentiful, became hopeless, and game scarcer than ever, the gentlemen waxed dull, and began to catch at the smallest amusements. They grew as excited as the little boys over nutting-parties, going in whole boat-loads to the other side of the loch, and promising to bring home large bags of nuts for winter consumption, but somehow the nuts all got eaten before the boats reached land.

The clergyman was often one of the nutting-party. He knew every nook and corner of the country round, was equally good at an oar or a fishing-rod, could walk miles upon miles across the mountains, and scramble over rocks as light as a deer. Besides, he was so kind to children, and took such pleasure in pleasing them, that he earned their deepest gratitude, as young things understand gratitude. But they are loving, any how, to those that love them, and to have those little boys climbing over him, and hanging about him, and teasing him on all occasions to give them "a low," was, I dare say, sufficient reward for the good minister.

Sunny liked him too, very much, and was delighted to go out with him. But there was such dangerous emulation between her and the boys in the matter of "fishing" for dead leaves, with a stick, which involved leaning over the boat's side, and snatching at them when caught, and mamma got so many frights, that she was not sorry when the minister announced that every nut-tree down the canal had been "harried" of its fruit, and henceforward people must content themselves with dry land and blackberries.

This was not an exciting sport, and one day the gentlemen got so hard up for amusement that they spent half the morning in watching some gymnastics of Maurice and Eddie, which consisted in climbing up to their papa's shoulder and sitting on his head. (A proceeding which Sunny admired so, that she never rested till she partly imitated it by "walking up mamma as if she was a tree," which she did at last like a little acrobat.)

Children and parents became quite interested in their mutual performances; every body laughed a good deal, and forgot to grumble at the weather, when news arrived that a photographer, coming through the glen, had stopped at the house, wishing to know if the family would like their portraits taken.

Now, any body, not an inhabitant, coming through the glen, was an object of interest in this lonely place. But a photographer! Maurice's papa caught at the idea enthusiastically.

"Have him in, by all means. Let us see his pictures. Let us have ourselves done in a general group."

"And the children," begged their mamma. "Austin Thomas has never been properly taken, and baby not at all. I must have a portrait of baby."   .

"Also," suggested somebody, "we might as well take a portrait of the mountains. They'll sit for it quiet enough; which is more than can be said for the children, probably."

It certainly was. Never had a photographer a more hard-working morning. No blame to the weather, which (alas, for the salmon-fishers!) was perfect as ever; but the difficulty of catching the sitters, and arranging them, and keeping them steady, was enormous.

First, the servants all wished to be taken; some separately, and then in a general group, which was arranged beside the kitchen door, the scullery being converted into a "dark room" for the occasion. One after the other, the maids disappeared, and re-appeared full-dressed, in the most wonderful crinolines and chignons, but looking not half so picturesque as a Highland farm-girl, who, in her woollen striped petticoat and short gown, with her dark red hair knotted up behind, sat on the wall of the yard, contemplating the proceedings.

The children ran hither and thither highly delighted, except Franky and Austin Thomas, who were made to suffer a good deal, the latter being put into a stiff white piqué frock, braided with black braid, which looked exactly as if some one had mistaken him for a sheet of letter-paper and begun to write upon him; while Franky, dressed in his Sunday's best, with his hair combed and face clean, was in an aggravating position for his ordinary week-day amusements. He consoled himself by running in and out among the servants, finally sticking himself in the centre of the group, and being depicted there, as natural as life.

A very grand picture it was, the men-servants being in front — Highland men always seem to consider themselves superior beings, and are seen lounging about and talking, while the women are shearing, or digging, or hoeing potatoes. The maids stood in a row behind, bolt upright, smiling as hard as they could, and little Franky occupied the foreground, placed between the gardener's knees. A very successful photograph, and worthy of going down to posterity, as doubtless it will.

Now for the children. The baby, passive in an embroidered muslin frock, came out, of course, as a white mass with something resembling a face at the top; but Austin Thomas was a difficult subject. He wouldn't sit still, no, not for a minute, but kept wriggling about on the kitchen chair that was brought for him, and looked so miserable in his stiff frock, that his expression was just as if he were going to be whipped, and didn't like it at all.

In vain Franky, who always patronized and protected his next youngest brother in the tenderest way, began consoling him, "Never mind, sonnie"—that was Franky's pet name for Austin—"they shan't hurt you. I'll take care they don't hurt you."

Still, the great black thing, with the round glass eye fixed upon him, was too much for Austin's feelings. He wriggled, and wriggled, and never would his likeness have been taken at all—at least, that morning—if somebody had not suggested "a piece." Off flew Mary the cook, and brought back the largest "piece"—

bread with lots of jam upon it—that ever little
Scotchman revelled in. Austin took it, and,
being with great difficulty made to understand
that he must pause in eating now and then,
the photographer seized the happy moment,
and took him between his mouthfuls, with
Franky keeping guard over him the while, lest
any body did him any harm. And a very
good picture it is, though neither boy is quite
handsome enough, of course. No photographs
ever are.

Little Sunshine, meanwhile, had been deeply
interested in the whole matter. She was quite
an old hand at it, having herself sat for her
photograph several times.

"Would you like to see my likenesses?" she
kept asking any body or every body; and
brought down the whole string of them, de-
scribing them one by one: "Sunny in her
mamma's arms, when she was a little baby,
very cross;" "Sunny just going to cry;"
"Sunny in a boat;" "Sunny sitting on a
chair;" "Sunny with her shoes and stockings
off, kicking over a basket;" and lastly (the
little show-woman always came to this with
a scream of delight), "That's my papa and
mamma, Sunny's own papa and mamma, both
together!"

L

Though, then, she had not been in the least afraid of the camera, but, when the great glass eye looked at her, looked steadily at it back, still she did not seem to like it now. She crept beside her mamma and her Lizzie, looking on with curiosity, but keeping a long way off, till the groups were done.

There were a few more taken, in one of which Sunny stood in the door-way in her Lizzie's arms. And her papa and mamma, who meanwhile had taken a good long walk up the hill-road, came back in time to figure in two rows of black dots on either side of a shady road, which were supposed to be portraits of the whole party. The mountains opposite also sat for their likenesses—which must have been a comfort to the photographer, as they at least could not "move." But, on the whole, the honest man made a good morning's work, and benefited considerably thereby.

Which was more than the household did. For, as was natural, the cook being dressed so beautifully, the dinner was left pretty much to dress itself. Franky and Austin Thomas suffered so much from having on their best clothes that they did not get over it for ever so long. And Sunny, too, upset by these irregular proceedings, when taking a long promised afternoon walk with her papa, was as cross as such a generally good little girl could be: insisting on being carried the whole way, and carried only by her mamma. And though, as mamma often says, " She wouldn't sell her for her weight in gold," she is a pretty considerable weight to carry on a warm afternoon.

Still the day had passed pleasantly away, the photographs were all- done, to remain as memorials of the holiday, long after it was ended. In years to come, when the children are all men and women, they may discover them in some nook or other, and try to summon up faint recollections of the time. Oh! if Little Sunshine might never cry except to be carried in mamma's arms! and Austin Thomas find no sorer affliction in life than sitting to be photographed in stiff white clothes! But that can not be. They must all bear their burdens, as their parents did. May God take care of them when we can do it no more!

The week had rolled by—weeks roll by so fast!—and it was again Sunday, the last Sunday at the glen, and just such another as before; calm, still, sunshiny: nothing but peace on earth and sky. Peace! when far away beyond the circle of mountains within which parents and children were enjoying such inno-

cent pleasures, such deep repose, there was going on, for other parents and children, the terrible siege of Paris. Week by week, and day
by day, the Germans were closing in round the
doomed city, making ready to destroy by fire,
or sword, or famine—all sent by man's hand,
not God's—hundreds, thousands of innocent
enemies. Truly, heaven will have been well
filled, and earth well emptied during the year
1870.

What a glorious summer it was, as to weather, will long be remembered in Scotland. Even
up to this Sunday, the 2d of October, the air
was balmy and warm as June. Every body
gathered outside on the terrace, including the
forlorn salmon-fishers, whose last hope was
now extinguished, for the patient gentleman,
and Sunny's papa, too, were to leave next
morning. And the fish jumped up in the
glassy loch, livelier than ever, as if they were
having a special jubilee in honor of their foe's
departure.

He sat resigned and cheerful, smoking his
cigar, and protesting that, with all his piscatory
disappointments, this was the loveliest place he
had ever been in, and that he had spent the
pleasantest of holidays! There he was left to
enjoy his last bit of the mountains and loch in

quiet content, while every body else went to church.

Even Little Sunshine. For her mamma and papa had taken counsel together whether it was not possible for her to be good there, so as at least to be no hindrance to other people's going, which was as much as could be expected for so small a child. Papa doubted this, but mamma pleaded for her little girl, and promised to keep her good if possible. She herself had a great desire that the first time ever Sunny went to church should be in this place.

So they had a talk together, mamma and Sunny, in which mamma explained that Sunny might go to church, as Maurice and Eddie did, if she would sit quite quiet, as she did at prayers, and promise not to speak one word, as nobody ever spoke in church excepting the minister. She promised, this little girl who has such a curious feeling about keeping a promise, and allowed herself to be dressed without murmuring—nay, with a sort of dignified pride—to "go to church." She even condescended to have her gloves put on, always a severe trial; and never was there a neater little figure, all in white from top to toe, with a white straw hat, as simple as possible,

and the yellow·curls tumbling down from under it. As she put·her little hand in her mamma's and they two started together, somewhat
in advance of the rest, for it was a long half-
mile for such baby-feet, her mamma involuntarily thought of a verse in a poem she learnt
when she herself was a little girl :

> "Thy dress was like the lilies,
> And thy heart was pure as they;
> One of God's holy angels,   .
> Did walk with me that day."

Only Sunny was not an angel, but an ordinary
little girl. A good little girl generally, but
capable of being naughty sometimes. She
will have to try hard to be good every day
of her life, as we all have. Still, with her
sweet grave face, and her soft pretty ways,
there was something of the angel about her
this day.

Her mamma tried to make her understand,
in a dim way, what "church" meant—that it
was saying "thank you!" to God, as mamma
did continually; especially for His giving her
her little daughter. How He lived up in the
sky, and nobody saw Him, but He saw every
body; how He loved Little Sunshine, just as
her papa and mamma loved her, and was glad
when she was good, and grieved when she was

naughty. This was all the child could possibly take in, and even thus much was doubtful; but she listened, seeming as if she com-
prehended a small fragment of the great mys-
tery which even we parents understand so little. Except that when we look at our children, and feel how dearly we love them, how
much we would both do and sacrifice for them,
how if we have to punish them it is never in
anger but in anguish and pain, suffering twice
as much ourselves the while—then we can
faintly understand how He who put such love
into us, must Himself love infinitely more, and
meant us to believe this, when He called Himself our Father. Therefore it was that through
her papa's and mamma's love Sunny could best
be taught her first dim idea of God.

She walked along very sedately, conversing
by the way, and not attempting to dart from
side to side, after one object or another, as this
butterfly child always does on a week-day.
But Sunday, and Sunday clothes, conduced exceedingly to proper behavior. Besides, she
felt that she was her mamma's companion, and
was proud accordingly. Until, just before
reaching the church, came a catastrophe which
certainly could not have happened in any other
church-going walk than this.

A huge, tawny-colored bull stood in the centre of the road, with half a dozen cows and calves behind him. They moved away, feeding leisurely on either side the road, but the bull held his ground, looking at mamma and Sunny from under his shaggy brows, as if he would like to eat them up.

"Mamma, take her!" whispered the poor little girl, rather frightened, but neither crying nor screaming.

Mamma popped her prayer-book in her pocket, dropped her parasol on the ground, and took up her child on her left arm, leaving the right arm free. A fortnight ago she would have been alarmed, but now she understood the ways of these Highland cattle, and that they were not half so dangerous as they looked. Besides, the fiercest animal will often turn before a steady, fearless human eye. So they stood still, and faced the bull, even Sunny meeting the creature with a gaze as firm and courageous as her mamma's. He stood it for a minute or so, then he deliberately turned tail, and walked up the hill-side.

"The big bull didn't hurt Sunny! He wouldn't hurt little Sunny, would he, mamma!" said she, as they walked on together. She has the happiest conviction that no crea-

ture in the world would ever be so unkind as
to hurt Sunny. How should it—when she is
never unkind to any living thing? When the
only living thing that ever she saw hurt—a
wasp that crept into the carriage, and stung
Sunny on her poor little leg, and her nurse
was so angry that she killed it on the spot—
caused the child a troubled remembrance.
She talked, months afterwards, with a grave
countenance, of "the wasp that was obliged to
be killed, because it stung Sunny."

She soon looked benignly at the big bull, now
standing watching her from the hill-side, and
wanted to play with the little calves, who still
staid feeding near. She was also very anxious to know if they were going to church
too? But before the question—a rather puz-
zling one—could be answered, she was over-
taken by the rest of the congregation, including
Maurice and Eddie, with their parents. The
two boys only smiled at her, and walked into
church, so good and grave that Sunny was im-
pressed into preternatural gravity too. When
the rest were seated, she, holding her mamma's
hand, walked quietly in as if accustomed to it
all, and joined the congregation.

The seat they chose was, for precaution, the
one nearest the door, and next to "*the* pauper,"

an old man who alone of all the inhabitants of
the glen did not work, but received parish relief. He was just able to come to church, but
looked as if he had "one foot in the grave," as
people say (whither, indeed, the other foot soon
followed, for the poor old man died not many
weeks after this Sunday). He had a wan,
weary, but uncomplaining face; and as the
rosy child, with her bright curls, her fair fresh
cheeks, and plûmp round limbs, sat down upon
the bench beside him, the two were a strange
and touching contrast.

Never did any child behave better than Little Sunshine, on this her first going to church.
Yes, even though she soon caught sight of her
own papa, sitting a few benches off, but afraid
to look at her lest she should misbehave.
Also of Maurice's papa and mamma, and of
Maurice and Eddie themselves, not noticing
her at all, and behaving beautifully. She saw
them, but, faithful to her promise, she did not
speak one word, not even in a whisper to mamma. She allowed herself to be lifted up and
down, to sit or stand as the rest did, and when
the music began she listened with an eçstasy
of pleasure on her little face; but otherwise
she conducted herself as well as if she had been
thirteen, instead of not quite three years old.

Once only, when the prayers were half through, and the church was getting warm, she gravely took off her hat and laid it on the bench before her—sitting the rest of the service with her pretty curls bare—but that was all.

During the sermon she was severely tried. Not by its length, for it was fortunately short, and she sat on her mamma's lap, looking fixedly into the face of the minister, as pleased with him in his new position as when he was rowing her in the boat, or gathering nuts for her along the canal bank. All were listening, as attentive as possible, for every body loved him, Sundays and week-days; and even Sunny herself gazed as earnestly as if she were taking in every word he said—when her quick little eyes were caught by a new interest—a small, shaggy Scotch terrier, who put his wise-looking head inquiringly in at the open door.

Oh, why was the church door left open? No doubt, so thought the luckless master of that doggie! He turned his face away; he kept as quiet as possible, hoping not to be discovered; but the faithful animal was too much for him. In an ecstasy of joy, the creature rushed in and out and under several people's legs, till he got to the young man who owned him, and then jumped upon him in unmistakable recognition. Happily, he did not bark; indeed, his master, turning red as a peony, held his hand over the creature's mouth.

What was to be done? If he scolded the dog, or beat him, there would be a disturbance immediately; if he encouraged or caressed him, the loving beast would have begun—in fact, he did slightly begin — a delighted whine. All the perplexed master could do was to keep him as quiet as circumstances allowed, which he managed somehow by setting his foot on the wildly-wagging tail, and twisting his fingers in one of the long ears, the dog resisting not at all. Quite content, if close to his master, the faithful beast snuggled down, amusing himself from time to time by gnawing first a hat, and then an umbrella, and giving one small growl as an accidental footstep passed down the road; but otherwise behaving as as well as any body in church. The master, too, tried to face out his difficulty, and listen as if nothing was the matter; but I doubt he rather lost the thread of the sermon.

So did Sunny's mamma for a few minutes. Sunny is so fond of little doggies, that she fully expected the child to jump from her lap, and run after this one; or, at least, to make a loud remark concerning it, for the benefit of the congregation generally. But Sunny evidently remembered that "nobody spoke in church;" and possibly she regarded the dog's entrance as a portion of the service, for she maintained the most decorous gravity. She watched him, of course, with all her eyes; and once she turned with a silent appeal to her mamma to look too, but said not a word. The little terrier himself did not behave better than she, to the very end of the service.

It ended with a beautiful hymn—"O Thou from whom all goodness flows." Every body knows it, and the tune too; which I think was originally one of those sweet litanies to the Virgin which one hears in French churches, especially during the month of May. The little congregation knew it well, and sang it well too. When Sunny saw them all stand up, she of her own accord stood up likewise, mounting the bench beside the old pauper, who turned half round, and looked on the pleasant child with a faint, pathetic sort of smile.

Strange it was to stand and watch the different people who stood singing, or listening to, that hymn; Maurice and Eddie, with their papa and mamma; other papas and mammas with their little ones; farmers and farm-serv-

ants who lived in the glen, with a chance
tourist or two who happened to be passing
through; several old Highland women, grim
and gaunt with long hard-working lives; the
poor old pauper, who did not know that his
life was so nearly over; and lastly, the little
three-years-old child, with her blue eyes wide
open and her rosy lips parted, not stirring a
foot or a finger, perfectly motionless with delight. · Verse after verse rose the beautiful
hymn, not the less beautiful because so familiar :

"O Thou from whom all goodness flows,
    I lift my soul fo Thee;
  In all my sorrows, conflicts, woes,
    O Lord, remember me!

"When on my aching burdened heart,
    My sins lie heavily,
  Thy pardon grant, Thy peace impart,
    In love, remember me!

"When trials' sore obstruct my way,
    And ills I can not flee,
  Oh! let my strength be as my day,
    For good, remember me!

"When worn with pain, disease, and grief,
    This feeble body see,
  Give patience, rest, and kind relief,
    Hear, and remember me!

" When in the solemn hour of death
   I wait Thy just decree,
Be this the prayer of my last breath,
   'O Lord, remember me!'"

As Little Sunshine stood there, unconscious·
ly moving her baby lips to the pretty tune—
ignorant of all the words and their meaning—
her mother, not ignorant, took the tiny soft
hand in hers and said for her in her heart,
"Amen."

When the hymn was done, the congregation
passed slowly out of church, most of them
stopping to speak or shake hands, for of course
all knew one another, and several were neigh-
bors and friends. Then at last Sunny's papa
ventured to take up his little girl, and kiss
her, telling her what a very good little girl she
had been, and how pleased he was to see it.
The minister, walking home between Maurice
and Eddie, who seized upon him at once,
turned round to say that he had never known
a little girl, taken to church for the first time,
behave so remarkably well. And though she
was too young to understand any thing except
that she had been a good girl, and every body
loved her and was pleased with her, still Sunny also looked pleased, as if satisfied that
church-going was a sweet and pleasant thing.

CHAPTER X.

L ITTLE SUNSHİNE'S delicious holiday —equally delicious to her papa and mamma too—was now fast drawing to a close. This Sunday sunset, more gorgeous perhaps than ever, was the last that the assembled party of big and little people watched together from the terrace. By the next Sunday, they knew, all of them would be scattered far and wide, in all human probability never again to meet, as a collective party, in this world. For some of them had come from the " under world," the Antipodes, and were going back thither in a few months, and all had their homes and fortunes widely dispersed, so as to make their chances of future reunion small.

They were sorry to part, I think—even those who were nearly strangers to one another—and those who were friends were very sorry indeed. The children, of course, were not sorry at all, for they understood nothing about the matter. For instance, it did not occur in the

least to Sunny or to Austin Thomas (still view-
ing one another with suspicious eyes, and always on the brink of war, though Sunny kept
her promise, and did not attack again), that the
next time they met might be as big boy and
girl, learning lessons, and not at all disposed
to fight; or else as grown young man and
woman, obliged to be polite to one another
whether they liked it or not.

But the elders were rather grave, and watched the sun set—or rather not the sun, for he
was always invisible early in the afternoon, the
house being placed on the eastern slope of the
hill—but the sunset glow on the range of
mountains opposite. Which, as the light gradually receded upward, the shadow pursuing,
had been evening after evening the loveliest
sight imaginable. This night especially, the
hills seemed to turn all colors, fading at last
into a soft gray, but keeping their outlines
distinct long after the loch and valley were left
dark.

So, good-bye, sun! When he rose again,
two of the party would be on board a steamboat—*the* steamboat, for there was but one—sailing away southward, where there were no hills,
no lochs, no salmon-fishing, no idle sunshiny
days—nothing but work, work, work. For

M

" grown-ups," as Sunny calls them, do really
work; though, as a little girl once observed
pathetically to Sunny's mamma, " Oh, I wish I
was grown up, and then I might be idle ! We
children have to work *so* hard ! while you and
my mamma do nothing all day long." (Oh
dear !)

Well, work is good, and pleasant too;
though perhaps Sunny's papa did not exactly
think so, when he gave her her good-night kiss,
which was also good-bye. For he was to start
so early in the morning that it was almost the
middle of the night, in order to catch the steamer which should touch at the pier ten miles
off, between six and seven A.M. Consequently,
there was breakfast by candle-light, and hasty
adieux, and a dreary departure of the carriage
under the misty morning starlight; every body
making an effort to be jolly, and not quite ac-
complishing it. Then every body or as many
as had had courage to rise, went to bed again,
and tried to sleep, with varied success, Sunny's
mamma with none at all.

It recurred to her, as a curious coincidence,
that this very day, twenty-five years before,
after sitting up all night, she had watched, solemnly as one never does it twice in a life-time,
a glorious sunrise. She thought she would go

out and watch another, from the hill-side, over the mountains.

My children, did you ever watch a sunrise? No? Then go and do it as soon as ever you can. Not lazily from your bed-room window, but out in the open air, where you seem to hear and see the earth gradually waking up, as she does morning after morning, each waking as wonderful and beautiful as if she had not done the same for thousands of years, and may do it for thousands more.

When the carriage drove off, it was still starlight—morning starlight, pale, dreary, and excessively cold; but now a faint colored streak of dawn began to put the stars out, and creep up and up behind the curves of the eastern hills. Gradually, the daylight increased—it was clear enough to see things, though every thing looked cheerless and gray. The grass and heather were not merely damp, but soaking wet; and over the loch and its low-lying shores was spread a shroud of white mist. There was something almost painful in the intense stillness; it felt as if all the world were dead and buried, and when suddenly a cock crew from the farm, he startled one as if he had been a ghost.

But the mountains—the mountains! Turning eastward, to look at them, all the dullness, solitude, and dreariness of the lower world vanished. They stood literally bathed in light, as the sun rose up behind them, higher and higher, brighter and brighter, every minute. Suddenly, an arrow of light shot across the valley; and touched the flat granite bowlder on which, after a rather heavy. climb; Sunny's mamma had succeeded in perching herself like a large bird, tucking her feet under her, and wrapping herself up as tightly as possible in her plaid, as some slight protection against the damp cold. But when the sunshine came, chilliness and cheerlessness vanished. And as. the beam broadened, it seemed to light up the whole world.

How she longed for her child, not merely for company, though that would have been welcome in the extreme solitude, but that she might show her, what even such baby eyes could not but have seen—the exceeding beauty of God's earth, and told her how it came out of the love of God, who loved the world and all that was in it. How He·loved Sunny, and would take care of her all her life, as He had taken care of her, and of her mamma, too. How, if she were good and loved Him back again, He would be sure to make for her,

through all afflictions, a happy life; since, like
the sunrise, " His mercies are new every morning, and His compassions fail not."

Warmer and warmer the cold rock grew; a
few birds began to twitter, the cocks crowed
from the farm-yard, and from one of the cot-
tages a slender line of blue peat-smoke crept
up, showing that somebody else was awake besides Sunny's mamma; which was rather a
comfort—she was getting tired of having the
world all to herself.

Presently an old woman came out of a cot-
tage-door, and went to the burn for water,
probably to make her morning porridge. A
tame sheep followed her, walking leisurely to
the burn and back again, perhaps with an eye
to the porridge-pot afterwards. And a lazy
pussy-cat also crept out, and climbed on the
roof of the cottage, for a little bit of sunshine
before breakfast. Sunny's mamma also began
to feel that it was time to see about breakfast,
for sunrise on the mountains makes one very
hungry.

Descending the hill was worse than ascending, there being no regular track, only some
marks of where the sheep were in the habit of
climbing. And the granite rocks presented a
flat sloping surface, sometimes bare, sometimes

covered with slippery moss, which was not too agreeable. Elsewhere, the ground was generally boggy, with tufts of heather between, which one might step or jump. But as soon as one came to a level bit it was sure to be bog, with little streams running through it, which had to be crossed somehow, even without the small convenience of stepping-stones.

Once, when her stout stick alone saved her from a sprained ankle, she amused herself with thinking how in such a case she might have shouted vainly for help, and how bewildered the old woman at the cottage would have been on finding out that the large creature, a sheep as she probably supposed, sitting on the bowlder overhead, which she had looked up at once or twice, was actually a wandering lady!

It was now half-past seven, and the usual breakfast party on the door-step was due at eight. Welcome was the sound of little voices, and the patter of small eager feet along the gravel walk. Sunny's mamma had soon her own child in her arms, and the other children round her, all eating bread and butter and drinking milk with the greatest enjoyment. The sun was now quite warm, and the mist had furled off the loch, leaving it clear and smooth as ever.

Suddenly Eddie's sharp eyes caught something there which quite interrupted his meal. It was a water-fowl, swimming in and out among the island of water-lilies, and even coming as close in shore as the pier. Not one of the nine geese, certainly; this bird was dark-colored, and small, yet seemed larger than the water-hens, which also were familiar to the children. Some one suggested it might possibly be a wild duck.

Eddie's eyes brightened, "Then might I 'low' in a boat, with papa's gun, and go and shoot it?"

This being a too irregular proceeding, Sunny's mamma proposed a medium course, namely, that Eddie should inform his papa that there was a bird supposed to be a wild duck, and then he might do as he thought best about shooting it.

Maurice and Eddie were accordingly off like lightning; three of Maurice's worms, which had taken the opportunity of crawling out of his pocket and on to the tray, being soon afterwards found leisurely walking over the bread and butter plate. Franky and Austin Thomas took the excitement calmly, the one thinking it a good chance of eating up his brothers' rejected shares, and the other proceeding unnoticed to his favorite occupation of filling the salt-cellar with sand from the walk.

Soon, Donald, who had also seen the bird, appeared, with his master's gun all ready, and the master having got into his clothes in preternaturally quick time, hurried down to the loch, his boys accompanying him. Four persons, two big and two little, after one unfortunate bird! which still kept swimming about, a tiny black dot on the clear water, as happy and unconscious as possible.

The ladies, too, soon came out and watched the sport from the terrace; wondering whether the duck was within range of the gun, and whether it really was a wild duck, or not. A shot, heard from behind the trees, deepened the interest; and when, a minute after, a boat containing Maurice, Eddie, their papa, and Donald, was seen to pull off from the pier, the excitement was so great that nobody thought about breakfast.

"It must be a wild duck; they have shot it: it will be floating on the water, and they are going after it in the boat."

"I hope Eddie will not tumble into the water, in his eagerness to pull the bird out."

"There—the gun is in the boat with them!

Suppose Maurice stumbles over it, and it goes off and shoots somebody."

Such were the maternal forebodings, but nothing of the sort happened, and by-and-by, when breakfast was getting exceedingly cold, a little procession, all unharmed, was seen to wind up from the loch, Eddie and Maurice on either side of their papa. He walked between them, shouldering his gun, so that loaded or not, it could not possibly hurt his little boys. But he looked extremely dejected, and so did Donald, who followed, bearing " the body "—of a poor little dripping, forlorn-looking bird. .

"Is that the wild duck?" asked every body at once.

" Pooh! It wasn't a wild duck at all. It was only a large water-hen. Not worth the trouble of shooting, certainly not of cooking. And then we had all the bother of getting out the gun, and tramping over the wet grass to get a fair shot, and, after we shot it, of rowing after it, to fish it up out of the loch. Wretched bird!"

Donald, imitating his master, regarded the booty with the utmost contempt, even kicking it with his foot as it lay, poor little thing! But no kicks could harm it now. Sunny only went up and touched it timidly, strok-

ing its pretty wet feathers with her soft little
hand. .

"Mamma, can't it fly? why doesn't it get up
and fly away? And it is so cold. Might
Sunny warm it?" as she had once tried to
warm the only dead thing she ever saw—a little field-mouse lying on the garden-walk at
home, which she put in her pinafore and cuddled up to her little "bosie," and carried about
with her for half an hour or more.

Quite puzzled, she watched Donald carrying
off the bird, and only half accepted mamma's
explanation that "there was no need to warm
it—it was gone to its bye-bye, and would not
wake up any more."

Though she was living at a shooting-lodge,
this was the only dead thing Sunny had yet
chanced to see, for there was so little game.
about that the gentlemen rarely shot any.
But this morning one of them declared that
if he walked his legs off over the mountains,
he must go and have a try at something. So
off he set, guided by Donald, while the rest of
the party fished meekly for trout, or went
along the hill-road on a still more humble
hunt after blackberries. Sometimes they won-
dered about the stray sportsman, and listened
for gun-shots from the hills—the sound of a

égorieЯ

gun could be heard for so very far in this still bright weather. And when at the usual dinner-hour he did not appear, they waited a little while for him. They were going at length to begin the meal, when he was seen coming leisurely along the garden walk.

Eager were the inquiries of the master. " Well—any grouse?"

" No."

"Partridges?"

" No."

"I knew it. There has not been a partridge seen here for years. Snipes, perhaps?"

" Never saw one."

" Then, what have you been about? Have you shot nothing at all?"

" Not quite nothing. A roe-deer. The first I ever killed in my life. Here, Donald."

With all his brevity, the sportsman could not hide the sparkle of his eye. Donald, looking equally delighted, unloosed the creature, which he had been carrying round his neck in the most affectionate manner, its fore legs clasped over one shoulder, and its hind legs over the other, and laid it down on the gravel walk.

What a pretty creature it was, with its round slender shapely limbs, its smooth satin skin, and its large eyes, that in life would have been so soft and bright! They were dim and glazed now, though it was scarcely cold yet.

Every body gathered round to look at it, and the sportsman told the whole story of his shot.

"She is a hind, you see; most likely has a fawn somewhere not far off. For I shot her close by the farm here. I was coming home, not over-pleased at coming so empty-handed, when I saw her standing on the hill-top, just over that rock there; a splendid shot she was, but so far off that I never thought I should touch her. However, I took aim, and down she dropped. Just feel her. She is an admirable creature, so fat! Quite a picture!"

So it was, but a rather sad one. The deer lay, her graceful head hopelessly dangling, and bloody drops beginning to ooze from her open mouth. Otherwise she might have been asleep —as innocent. Sunny, who had run with the boys to see the sight, evidently thought she was.

"Mamma, look at the little baa-lamb, the dear little baa-lamb. Won't it wake up?"

• Mamma explained that it was not a baa-lamb, but a deer, and there stopped, considering how to make her child understand that

solemn thing, death; which no child can be
long kept in ignorance of, and yet which is so
difficult to explain. Meantime, Sunny stood
looking at the deer, but did not attempt to
touch it as she had touched the water-hen. It
was so large a creature to lie there so helpless
and motionless. At last she looked up, with
trouble in her eyes.

"Mamma, it won't wake up. Make it wake
up, please!"

"I can't, my darling!" And there came a
choke in mamma's throat—this foolish mamma,
who dislikes "sport"—who looks upon soldiers as man-slayers, "glory" as a great delusion, and war a heinous crime. "My little one,
the pretty deer has gone to sleep, and nobody
can wake it up again. But it does not suffer.
Nothing hurts it now. Come away, and
mamma will tell you more about this another day."

The little fingers contentedly twined themselves in her mamma's, and Sunshine came
away, turning back now and then a slightly
regretful look on the poor hind that lay there,
the admiration of every body, and especially
of the gentleman who had shot it.

"The first I ever shot," he repeated, with
great pride. "I only wish I could stay and

eat her. But the rest of you will." (Except Sunny's mamma, who was rather glad to be spared that satisfaction.)

A single day was now all that remained of the visit—a day which dawned finer than ever, making it so hard to quit the hills, and the loch, and all the charms of this beautiful place. Not a cloud on the sky, not a ripple on the waters, blackberries saying " come gather me," by hundreds from every bramble, ferns of rare sort growing on dikes, and banks, and roots of trees. This whole morning must be spent on the hill-side by Sunny and her mamma, combining business with pleasure, if possible.

So they took a kitchen-knife as an extempore spade; a basket, filled with provisions, but meant afterwards to carry roots, and the well-known horn cup, which was familiar with so many burns. Sunny used it for all sorts of purposes besides drinking; filled it with pebbles, blackberries, and lastly with some doubtful vegetables, which she called " ferns," and dug up, and brought to her mamma to take home " very carefully."

Ere long she was left to mamma's charge entirely, for this was the last day, and Lizzie had never climbed a mountain, which she was most anxious to do, having the common delusion that to climb a mountain is the easiest thing in the world—as it looks, from the bottom.

Off she started, saying she should be back again directly, leaving mamma and the child to watch her from the latest point where there was a direct path—the cottage where the old woman had come out and gone to the burn at sunrise. Behind it was a large bowlder, sunshiny and warm to sit on, sheltered by a hay-rick, on the top of which was gambolling a pussy-cat. Sunny, with her usual love for animals, pursued it with relentless affection, and at last caught it in her lap, where it remained about one minute, and then darted away. Sunny wept bitterly, but was consoled by a glass of milk kindly brought by the old woman; with which she tried to allure pussy back again, but in vain.

So there was nothing for it but to sit on her mamma's lap and watch her Lizzie climbing up the mountain, in sight all the way, but gradually diminishing to the size of a calf, a sheep, a rabbit; finally of a black speck, which a sharp eye could distinguish moving about on the green hill-side, creeping from bush to bush, and from bowlder to bowlder, till at last it came to the foot of a perpendicular rock.

"She'll no climb that," observed the old woman, who had watched the proceeding with much interest. "Naebody ever does it: she'd better come down. Cry on her to come down."

"Will she hear?"

"Oh, yes."

And in the intense stillness, also from the law of sound ascending, it was curious how far one could hear. To mamma's great relief, the black dot stopped in its progress.

"Lizzie, come down," she called again, slowly and distinctly, and in a higher key, aware that musical notes will reach far beyond the speaking voice. "You've lost the path. Come down!"

"I'm coming," was the faint answer, and in course of time Lizzie came, very tired, and just a little frightened. She had begun to climb cheerfully and rapidly at first, for the hill-side looked in the distance nearly as smooth as an English field. When she got there, she found it was rather different—that heather-bushes, bowlders, mosses, and bogs, were not the pleasantest walking. Then she had to scramble on all-fours, afraid to look downward, lest her head should turn dizzy, and she might lose her hold, begin rolling and rolling, and never stop

till she came to the bottom. Still, she went
on resolutely, her stout English heart not lik-
ing to be beaten even by a Scotch mountain;
clinging from bush to bush—at this point a
small wood had grown up—until she reached
a spot where the rock was perpendicular, nay,
overhanging, as it formed the shoulder of the
hill.

"I might as well have climbed up the side
of 'a house," said poor Lizzie, forlornly; and
looked up at it, vexed at being conquered, but
evidently thankful that she had got down
alive. "Another time—or if I have somebody with me—I do believe I could do it."

Bravo, Lizzie! Half the doings in the world
are done in this spirit. Never say die! Try
again. Better luck next time.

Meanwhile she drank the glass of milk offered by the sympathizing old Highland woman, who evidently approved of the adventurous
English girl, then sat down to rest beside Little Sunny.

But Sunny had no idea of resting. She
never has, unless in bed and asleep. Now
she was bent upon also climbing a mountain—
a granite bowlder about three feet high.

"Look, mamma, look at Sunny! Sunny's
going to climb a mountain, like Lizzie."

N

Up she scrambled with both arms and legs—
catching at the edges of the bowlder, but tumbling back again and again. Still she was not
daunted.

"Don't help me!—don't help me!"·she kept
saying. "Sunny wants to climb a mountain
all by her own self."

Which feat she accomplished at last, and
succeeded in· standing upright on the top of
the bowlder, very hot, very tired, but triumph-
ant.

"Look, mamma! look at Sunny! Here she
is!"   •

Mamma looked; in fact, had been looking
out of the corner of her eye the whole time;
though not assisting at all in the courageous
effort.

"Yes, I see. Sunny has climbed a mountain: Clever little girl! Mamma is so pleased!"

How many "mountains" will she climb in her
life, that brave little soul! Mamma wonders
often, but knows not. Nobody knows.

In the mean time success was won. She,
her mamma, and her Lizzie, had each "climbed
a mountain." But they all agreed that though
pleasant enough in its way, such a performance
was a thing not to be attempted every day.

CHAPTER XI.

THE last day came—the last hour. Sunny,
her mamma, and her Lizzie, had to turn
their ways homeward—a long, long journey of
several hundred miles. To begin it at four in
the morning, with a child, too, was decided as
impracticable; so it was arranged that they
should leave over-night, and sleep at the only
available place, an inn which English superi-
ority scornfully termed a "public-house," but
which here in the Highlands was called the
"hotel," where "gentlemen could be accom-
modated with excellent shooting - quarters."
Therefore, it was supposed to be able to ac-
commodate a lady and a child—for one night
at least.

Fortunately, the shooting gentlemen did not
avail themselves of it; for the hotel contained
only two guest-rooms. These being engaged,
and the exact time of the boat next morning
learnt—which was not so easy, as every body
in the neighborhood gave different advice, and
a different opinion—the departure was settled.

Lovelier than ever looked the hills and the loch when the carriage came round to the door. All the little boys crowded round it with vociferous farewell—which they evidently thought great fun—Sunny likewise.

"Good-bye! good-bye!" cried she, as cheerfully as if it had been " how d'ye do," and obstinately refused to be kissed by any body. Indeed, this little girl does not like kisses, unless she offers them of her own accord.

One only grief she had, but that was a sharp one. Maurice's papa, who had her in his arms, suddenly proposed that they should "send mamma away, and keep Sunny;" and the scream of agony she gave, and the frantic way she clung to her mamma, and would not look at any body for fear of being kept prisoner, was quite pathetic.

At last the good-byes were over. For Little Sunshine these are as yet meaningless; life to her is a series of delight—the new ones coming as the old ones go. The felicity of kissing her hand and driving away, was soon followed by the amusement of standing on her mamma's lap, where she could see every thing along the road, which she had passed a fortnight before in dark night.

Now it was golden twilight—such a twi-

light! A year or two hence Sunny would
have been in ecstasy at the mountains, standing range behind range, literally transfigured
in light, with the young moon floating like a
"silver boat" (only turned the wrong way up-
permost) over their tops. As it was, the large
distant world interested her less than the small
near one—the trees that swept her face as she
drove along the narrow road, and the numerous cows and calves that fed on either side
of it.

There was also a salt-water loch, with fishing-boats drawn up on the beach, and long
fishing-nets hanging on poles; but not a living
creature in sight, except a heron or two. These
stood on one leg, solemnly, as herons do, and
then flew off, flapping their large wings with a
noise that made Little Sunshine, as she expressed it, "nearly jump." Several times, indeed, she "nearly jumped" out of the carriage
at the curious things she saw: such funny
houses, such little windows—"only one pane,
mamma"—and above all, the girls and boys
barefooted, shock-headed, that hung about star-
ing at the carriage as it passed.

"Have those little children got no Lizzie to
comb their hair?" she anxiously inquired; and
mamma was obliged to confess that probably

they had not, at which Sunny looked much surprised.

It was a long, long drive, even with all these entertainments; and before it ended, the twilight had faded, the moon crept higher over the hill, and Sunshine asked in a whisper for "Maymie's apron." The little "Maymie's apron," which had long lain in abeyance, was produced, and she soon snuggled down in her mamma's arms and fell fast asleep.

When she woke up the "hotel" was reached. Such a queer hotel! You entered by a low door-way, which opened into the kitchen below, and a narrow staircase leading to the guest-rooms above. From the kitchen Sunny heard a baby cry. She suddenly stopped, and would not go a step till mamma had promised she should see the baby — a very little baby, only a week old. Then she mounted with dignity up the rickety stairs, and began to examine her new apartments.

They were only two, and as homely as they well could be. Beside the sitting-room was a tiny bed-room, with a "hole in the wall," where Lizzie was to sleep. This "hole in the wall" immediately attracted Sunny; she jumped in it, and began crawling about it, and tried to stand upright under it, which, being such a

very little person, she was just able to do.
Finally, she wanted to go to sleep in it, till,
hearing she was to sleep with mamma, a much
grander thing, she went up to the bed, and in-
vestigated it with great interest likewise. Also
the preparations for her bath, which was to be
in a washing-tub in front of the parlor fire—a
peat fire. It had a delicious, aromatic smell,
and it brightened up the whole room, which
was very clean and tidy, after all.

So was the baby, which shortly appeared
in its mother's arms. She was a pale, delicate
woman, speaking English with the slow pre-
cision of a Highlander, and having the self-
composed, courteous manner that all High-
landers have. She looked much pleased when
her baby was admired—though not by Sunny,
who, never having seen so young a baby before, did not much approve of it, and especially disapproved of seeing it taken into her own
mamma's arms. So presently it and its mother disappeared, and Sunny and her mamma
were left to eat their supper of milk, bread
and butter, and eggs; which they did with
great content. Sunny was not quite so content to go to bed, but cried a little, till her
mamma set the parlor-door half open, that the
fire-light might shine in. Very soon she also

crept in beside her little girl; who was then not afraid of any thing.

But when they woke, in the dim dawn, it was under rather "frightening" circumstances. There was a noise below, of a most extraordinary kind, shouting, singing, dancing—yes, evidently dancing, though at that early hour of the morning. It could not have been continued from overnight, mamma having distinctly heard all the family go to bed, the children tramping loudly up the stairs, at nine o'clock, after which the inn was quite quiet. No, these must be new guests, and very noisy guests too. They stamped, they beat with their feet, they cried "whoop!" or "hech!" or some other perfectly unspellable word, at regular intervals. Going to sleep again was impossible; especially as Sunny, unaccustomed to such a racket, began to cry, and would have fallen into a downright sobbing fit, but for the amusement of going to the "hole in the wall," to wake her Lizzie. Upon which every body rose, the peat fire was rekindled, and the new day began.

The good folk below stairs must have begun it rather early. They were a marriage party who had walked over the hills, several miles, to see the bride and bridegroom off by the boat.

"Sunny wants to look at them," said the child, who listens to every thing, and wants to have a finger in every pie.

So, as soon as dressed, she was taken down, and stood at the door in her mamma's arms to see the fun.

Very curious "fun" it was. About a dozen young men and women, very respectable-looking, and wonderfully dressed, though the women had their muslin skirts pretty well draggled —not surprising, considering the miles they had trudged over mountain and bog, in the damp dawn of the morning—were dancing with all their might and main, the lassies with their feet, the lads with feet, heads, hands, tongues, snapping their fingers and crying "hech!" or whatever it was, in the most exciting manner. It was only excitement of dancing, however; none of them seemed the least drunk. They stopped a minute, at sight of the lady and child, and then went on again, dancing most determinedly, and as solemnly as if it were to save their lives, for the next quarter of an hour.

English Lizzie, who had never seen a Highland reel before, looked on with as much astonishment as Sunny herself. That small person, elevated in her mamma's arms, gazed on

the scene without a single smile; there being
no music, the dance was to her merely a noise
and a scuffle. Presently she said gravely,
" Now Sunny will go away."

They went away, and after drinking a glass
of milk—oh, what delicious milk those Highland cows give!—they soon heard the distant
paddles of the boat, as she steamed in between
the many islands of which this sea is full.
Then mounting an extraordinary vehicle, which
in the bill was called a "carridge," they headed
a procession, consisting of the wedding party
walking sedately two and two, a young man
and young woman arm in arm, down to the
pier. The married couple were put on board
the boat (together with Sunny, her mamma,
and her Lizzie, who all felt very small, and of
no consequence whatever), then there was a
great shouting and waving of handkerchiefs,
and a spluttering and splattering of Gaelic
good wishes, and the vessel sailed away.

By this time it was broad daylight, though
no sun was visible. Indeed, the glorious sun-
rises seemed ended now; it was a gray, cheerless morning, and so misty that no mountains
could be seen to take farewell of. The delicious Highland life was all gone by like a
dream.

This homeward journey was over the same route that Sunny had travelled a fortnight before, and she went through it in much the same fashion. She ran about the boat, and made friends with half a dozen people, for no kindly face is long a strange face to Little Sunshine. She was noticed even by the grim weather-beaten captain (he had a lot of little people of his own, he said), only when he told her she was "a bonnie wee lassie," she once more indignantly repelled the accusation.

"I'm not a bonnie wee lassie. I'm Sunny, mamma's little Sunny," repeated she, and would not look at him for at least two minutes.

She bore the various changes from sea-boat to canal-boat, etc., with her usual equanimity. At one place there was a great crush, and they got so squeezed up in a crowd that her mamma did not like it at all, but Sunny was perfectly composed, mamma's arms being considered protection against any thing. And when the nine locks came, she cheerfully disembarked and walked along the towing-path for half a mile, in the bravest manner. Gradually, as amusement began to fail her, she found several playfellows on board, a little dog tied by a string, and a pussy cat shut up in a hamper, which formed part of the luggage of an unfor-

tunate gentleman travelling to London with
five daughters, six servants, and about fifty
boxes—for he was overheard counting them.
In the long, weary transit between the canal-
boat and the sea, Sunny followed this impris-
oned cat, which mewed piteously; and in its
sorrows she forgot her own.

But she was growing very tired, poor child!
and the sunshine, which always has a curious
effect upon her temper and spirits, had now
altogether disappeared. A white, dull, chill
mist hung over the water, fortunately not thick
enough to stop traffic, as had happened two
days before, but still enough to make the river
very dreary. Little Sunshine, too, went under
a cloud; she turned naughty, and insisted on
doing whatever she was bid not to do; climbing in the most dangerous places, leaning over
the boat's side to look at the waves; misbe-
havior which required a strong hand and watch-
ful eyes to prevent serious consequences. But
mamma was more sorry than angry, for it was
hard for the little woman; and she was especially touched when, being obliged to forbid
some stale unwholesome fruit and doubtful
"sweeties," over which Sunny lingered and
longed, by saying "they belonged to the captain," the child answered sweetly,

"But if the kind captain were to give Sunny some, then she might have them?"

The kind captain not appearing, alas! she passed the basket with a sigh, and went down to the engines. To see the gigantic machinery turning and turning, never frightened but only delighted her. And mamma was so thankful to find any thing to break the tedium of the fourteen hours' journey, that though her little girl went down to the engine-room neat and clean in a white pelisse, and came up again looking just like a little sweep, she did not mind it at all!

Daylight faded; the boat emptied gradually of its passengers, including the gentleman with the large family and the fifty boxes; and on deck it began to grow very cold. Sunny had made excursions down below for breakfast, dinner, and tea, at all of which meals she conducted herself with the utmost propriety, but now she took up her quarters permanently in the comfortable saloon.

Not to sleep, alack! though her mamma settled down in a corner, and would have given any thing for "just one little minute," as Sunny says, of quiet slumber, but the child was now preternaturally wide awake, and as lively as a cricket. So was a little boy, named Willie, with whom she had made friends, and was on such terms of intimacy that they sat on the floor and shared their food together, and then jumped about, playing at all sorts of games, and screaming with laughter, so that even the few tired passengers who remained in the boat, as she steamed up the narrow, foggy river, could not help laughing too.

This went on for the space of two hours more, and even then, Sunny, who was quite good now, was with difficulty caught and dressed, in preparation for the stopping of the boat, when she was promised she should see papa. But she will endure any martyrdom of bonnet-tying or boot-buttoning if only she thinks she is going to meet her papa.

Unluckily there had been some mistake as to hours, and when she was carried on deck, in the sudden darkness, broken only by the glimmer of the line of lights along the wharf, and plunged into the midst of a dreadful confusion —porters leaping on board and screaming to passengers, and passengers searching wildly for their luggage—no papa was there. To double her grief, she also lost her mamma, who of course had to see to things at once herself. Through the noise and · whirl she heard the voice of the child, "Mamma! mamma!" It was a cry not merely of distress—but agony, with a "grown-up" tone in it of actual despair. No doubt the careless jest of Maurice's papa had rankled in her little mind, and she thought mamma was torn from her in real truth, and forever.

When at last mamma came back, the grasp with which the poor little girl clung to her neck was absolutely frantic.

"Mamma went away and left Sunny—Sunny lost mamma," and mamma could feel the little frame shaking with terror and anguish. Poor lamb! there was nothing to be done but to take her and hold her tight, and stagger with her somehow across the gangway to the cab. But even there she never loosened her clasp for a minute till she got safe into a bright warm house, where she found her own papa. Then the little woman was content.

She had still another journey before her, and without her papa too. A night journey, which promised to be easy and comfortable, but turned out quite the contrary. A journey in which Sunny's powers of endurance were taxed to the utmost, so that it will be years before she forgets the wind-up of her holiday.

Her papa put his family safe in a carriage all to themselves, and under special charge of the guard. Then he left them, just settling down to sleep; Sunny being disposed of in a snug corner, with an air-cushion for a pillow, and furry shawls wrapped about her, almost as cozy as in her own little crib, in which, after her various changes and vicissitudes, she was soon to repose once more.

She fell asleep in five minutes, and her mamma, who was very tired, soon dozed also, until roused by a sharp cry of fright. There was the poor little girl, lying at the bottom of the carriage, having been thrown there by its violent rocking. It rocked still, and rocked for many many miles, in the most dreadful manner. When it stopped the guard was appealed to, who said it was " the coupling-chains too slack," and promised to put all right. So the travellers went to sleep again, this time Sunny in her mamma's arms, which she refused to quit.

Again more jolting, and another catastrophe; mamma and the child finding themselves lying both together on the floor. This time Sunny was much frightened, and screamed violently, repulsing even her mamma.

"I thought you were not my own mamma; I thought you were somebody else," said she afterwards, and it was a long time before she came to her right self and cuddled down; the oscillation of the carriage continuing so bad that it was as much as her mamma could do, by wrapping her own arms round her, to protect the poor child from being hurt and bruised.

The guard, again appealed to, declared there was no danger, and that he would find a more comfortable carriage at the next stopping-place: but in vain. It was a full train, and the only two seats vacant were in a carriage full of gentlemen, who might object to a poor, sleepy, crying child. The little party went hopelessly back.

"Perhaps those gentlemen might talk so loud they might waken Sunny," said the child sagely, evidently remembering her experiences of five weeks ago. At any rate, nobody wished to try the experiment.

Since there was no actual danger, the only remedy was endurance. Mamma settled herself as firmly as she could, making a cradle of her arms. There, at length, the poor child, who had long ceased crying, and only gave an occasional weary moan, fell into a doze, which ended in quiet sleep. She was very heavy, and the hours seemed very long, but still they slipped away somehow. Nothing is absolute-

O

ly unbearable when one feels that, being inevitable, it must be borne.

Of course nobody slept, except the child, until near day-break, when a new and more benevolent guard came to the rescue, had the
coupling-chains fastened (which, they found,
had never been done at all till now), and less-
ened the shaking of the carriage. Then tired
Lizzie dropped asleep too, and the gray morning dawned upon a silent carriage, sweeping
rapidly across the level English country, so
different from that left behind. No more
lochs, no more mountains. No more sunshine
neither, as it appeared; for there was no sign
of sunrise, and the day broke amidst pelting
rain, which kept drip, drip, upon the top of the
carriage, till it seemed as if a deluge would
soon be added to the troubles of the journey.

But these were not so bad now. Very soon
the little girl woke up, neither frightened nor
cross, but the same sunshiny child as ever.

"Mamma!" she said, and smiled her own
·beaming smile, and sat up and looked about
her. "It's daylight. Sunny wants to get up."

That getting up was a most amusing affair.
It lasted as long as mamma's ingenuity could
possibly make it last, without any assistance
from poor worn-out Lizzie, who was left to

sleep her fill. First, Sunny's face and hands had to be washed with a damp sponge, and wiped with mamma's pocket - handkerchief. Then her hair was combed and brushed, with a brush that had a looking-glass on the back of it; in which she contemplated herself from time to time, laughing with exceeding merriment. Lastly, there was breakfast to be got ready, and eaten.

A most original breakfast! Beginning with a large pear, out of a basketful which a kind old gentleman had made up as a special present to Sunny; then some ham sandwiches—from which the ham was carefully extracted; then a good drink of milk. To uncork the bottle in which this milk had been carried, and pour it into the horn cup without spilling, required an amount of skill and care which occupied both mamma and Sunny for ever so long. In fact, they spent over their dressing and breakfasting nearly an hour; and by this time they were both in the best of spirits, and benignly compassionate to Lizzie, who slept on, and wanted no breakfast.

And when the sun at last came out, a watery and rather melancholy orb, not at all like the sun of the Highlands, the child was as bright and merry as if she had not travelled at all, and played about in the railway-carriage just as if it were her own nursery. .

This was well, for several weary hours had still to be passed ; the train was far behind its time; and what poor mamma would have done without the unfailing good temper of her "sunshiny child," she could not tell. When London was reached, and the benevolent guard once more put his head into the carriage, with "Here we are at last. I should think you'd had enough of it, ma'am," even he could not help giving a smile to the "little Missy" who was so merry and so good.

In London was an hour or two more of weary delay; but it was under a kindly roof, and Sunny had a second beautiful breakfast, all proper, with tea-cups and a table-cloth; which she did not seem to find half so amusing. as the irregular one in the railway-carriage. But she was very happy, and continued happy, telling all her adventures in Scotland to a dear old Scotchwoman whom she loves exceedingly, and who loves her back again. And being happy, she remained perfectly good, until once more put into a "puff-puff," to be landed at her own safe home.

Home. Even the child understood the joy of going home. She began talking of, "Sunny's nursery;" "Sunny's white pussy;" "Sunny's little dog Rose;" and recalling all the servants by name, showing she forgot nothing and nobody, though she had been absent so long. She chattered all the way down, till some ladies who were in the carriage could hardly believe she had been travelling all night. And when the train stopped, she was the first to look out of the window and call out "There's godmamma!"

So it was! Sunny's own kind godmamma, come unexpectedly to meet her and her tired mamma at the station; and oh! they were both so glad!

"Glad" was a small word to express the perfect and entire felicity of getting home—of finding the house looked just as usual; that the servants' cheerful faces beamed welcome; that even the doggie Rose barked, and white pussy purred, as if both were glad Little Sunshine was back again. She marched up stairs, lifting her short legs deliberately one after the other, and refusing to be carried ; then ran into her nursery, just as if she had left it only yesterday. And she "allowed" her mamma to have dinner with her there, sitting at table, as grand as if she were giving a dinner-party; and chattering like a little magpie to the very end of the meal.

But after that she collapsed. So did her mamma. So did her Lizzie. They were all so dreadfully tired that human nature could endure no more. Though it was still broad daylight, and with all the delights of home around them, they went to bed, and slept straight on—mamma "all round the clock," and the child and her Lizzie for fourteen hours!

Thus ended Little Sunshine's Holiday. It is told just as it happened, to amuse other little people, who no doubt are as fond as she is of hearing "stories." Only this is not a story, but the real truth. Not the whole truth, of course, for that would be breaking in upon what grown-up people term "the sanctities of private life." But there is no single word in it which is *not* true. I hope you will like it, little people, simple as it is. And so, good-bye!

THE END.

ABBOTTS' JUVENILE BOOKS.

THE FRANCONIA STORIES.

By JACOB ABBOTT. In Ten Volumes. Beautifully Illustrated. 16mo, Cloth, 90 cents per Vol.; the set complete, in case, $9 00.

Each volume is a distinct and independent work, having no necessary connection of incidents with those that precede or follow it, while yet the characters, and the scenes in which the stories are laid, are the same in all. They present pleasing pictures of happy domestic life, and are intended not only to amuse and entertain the children who shall peruse them, but to furnish them with attractive lessons of moral and intellectual instruction, and to train their hearts to habits of ready and cheerful subordination to duty and law.

1. **Malleville.**
2. **Mary Bell.**
3. **Ellen Linn.**
4. **Wallace.**
5. **Beechnut.**
6. **Stuyvesant.**
7. **Agnes.**
8. **Mary Erskine.**
9. **Rodolphus.**
10. **Caroline.**

YOUNG CHRISTIAN SERIES.

By JACOB ABBOTT. In Four Volumes. Richly Illustrated with Engravings, and Beautifully Bound. 12mo, Cloth, $1 75 per Vol. The set complete, Cloth, $7 00; in Half Calf, $14 00.

1. **The Young Christian.**
2. **The Corner Stone.**
3. **The Way to Do Good.**
4. **Hoaryhead and M'Donner.**

It is superfluous to speak of the rare merits of Mr. Abbott's writings on the subject of practical religion. Their extensive circulation, not only in our own country, but in England, Scotland, Ireland, France, Germany, Holland, India, and at various missionary stations throughout the globe, evinces the excellence of their plan, and the felicity with which it has been executed. In unfolding the different topics which he takes in hand, Mr. Abbott reasons clearly, concisely, and to the point; but the severity of the argument is always relieved by a singular variety and beauty of illustration. It is this admirable combination of discussion with incident that invests his writings with an almost equal charm for readers of every diversity of age and culture.

HARPER'S STORY BOOKS.

A Series of Narratives, Biographies, and Tales, for the Instruction and Entertainment of the Young. By JACOB ABBOTT. Embellished with more than One Thousand beautiful Engravings. Square 4to, complete in 12 large Volumes, or 36 small ones.

"HARPER'S STORY BOOKS" can be obtained complete in Twelve Volumes, bound in blue and gold, each one containing Three Stories, for $21 00, or in Thirty-six thin Volumes, bound in crimson and gold, each containing One Story, for $32 40. The volumes may be had separately—the large ones at $1 75 each, the others at 90 cents each.

VOL. I.

BRUNO; or, Lessons of Fidelity, Patience, and Self-Denial Taught by a Dog.

WILLIE AND THE MORTGAGE: showing How Much may be Accomplished by a Boy.

THE STRAIT GATE; or, The Rule of Exclusion from Heaven.

VOL. II.

THE LITTLE LOUVRE; or, The Boys' and Girls' Picture-Gallery.

PRANK; or, The Philosophy of Tricks and Mischief.

EMMA; or, The Three Misfortunes of a Belle.

VOL. III.

VIRGINIA; or, A Little Light on a Very Dark Saying.

TIMBOO AND JOLIBA; or, The Art of Being Useful.

TIMBOO AND FANNY; or, The Art of Self-Instruction.

VOL. IV.

THE HARPER ESTABLISHMENT; or, How the Story Books are Made.

FRANKLIN, the Apprentice-Boy.

THE STUDIO; or, Illustrations of the Theory and Practice of Drawing, for Young Artists at Home.

VOL. V.

THE STORY OF ANCIENT HISTORY, from the Earliest Periods to the Fall of the Roman Empire.

THE STORY OF ENGLISH HISTORY, from the Earliest Periods to the American Revolution.

THE STORY OF AMERICAN HISTORY, from the Earliest Settlement of the Country to the Establishment of the Federal Constitution.

VOL. VI.

JOHN TRUE; or, The Christian Experience of an Honest Boy.

ELFRED; or, The Blind Boy and his Pictures.

THE MUSEUM; or, Curiosities Explained. •

VOL. VII.

THE ENGINEER; or, How to Travel in the Woods.

RAMBLES AMONG THE ALPS.

THE THREE GOLD DOLLARS; or, An Account of the Adventures of Robin Green.

VOL. VIII.

THE GIBRALTAR GALLERY: being an Account of various Things both Curious and Useful.

THE ALCOVE: containing some Farther Account of Timboo, Mark, and Fanny.

DIALOGUES for the Amusement and Instruction of Young Persons.

VOL. IX.

THE GREAT ELM; or, Robin Green and Josiah Lane at School.

AUNT MARGARET; or, How John True kept his Resolutions.

VERNON; or, Conversations about Old Times in E. gl.nd.

VOL. X.

CARL AND JOCKO; or, The Adventures of the Little Italian Boy and his Monkey.

LAPSTONE; or, The Sailor turned Shoemaker.

ORKNEY, THE PEACEMAKER; or, The Various Ways of Settling Disputes.

VOL. XI.

JUDGE JUSTIN; or, The Little Court of Morningdale.

MINIGO; or, The Fairy of Cairnstone Abbey.

JASPER; or, The Spoiled Child Recovered.

VOL. XII.

CONGO; or, Jasper's Experience in Command.

VIOLA and her Little Brother Arno.

LITTLE PAUL; or, How to be Patient in Sickness and Pain.

Some of the Story Books are written particularly for girls, and some for Boys, and the different Volumes are adapted to various ages, so that the work forms a *Complete Library of Story Books* for all the Children of the Family and the Sunday-School. •

ABBOTTS' ILLUSTRATED HISTORIES.

Biographical Histories. By Jacob Abbott and John S. C. Abbott. The Volumes of this Series are printed and bound uniformly, and are embellished with numerous Engravings. 16mo, Cloth, $1 20 per volume. Price of the set (30 vols.), $36 00.

A series of volumes containing severally full accounts of the lives, characters, and exploits of the most distinguished sovereigns, potentates, and rulers that have been chiefly renowned among mankind, in the various ages of the world, from the earliest periods to the present day..

The successive volumes of the series, though they each contain the life of a single individual, and constitute thus a distinct and independent work, follow each other in the main, in regular historical order, and each one continues the general narrative of history down to the period at which the next volume takes up the story; so that the whole series presents to the reader a connected narrative of the line of general history from the present age back to the remotest times.

The narratives are intended to be succinct and comprehensive, and are written in a very plain and simple style. They are, however, not juvenile in their character, nor intended exclusively for the young. The volumes are sufficiently large to allow each history to comprise all the leading facts in the life of the personage who is the subject of it, and thus to communicate all the information in respect to him which is necessary for the purposes of the general reader.

Such being the design and character of the works, they would seem to be specially adapted, not only for family reading, but also for district, town, school, and Sunday-school libraries, as well as for text-books in literary seminaries.

The plan of the series, and the manner in which the design has been carried out by the author in the execution of it, have been highly commended by the press in all parts of the country. The whole series has been introduced into the school libraries of several of the largest and most influential states.

Abraham Lincoln's Opinion of Abbotts' Histories.—*In a conversation with the President just before his death, Mr. Lincoln said:* "*I want to thank you and your brother for Abbotts' series of Histories. I have not education enough to appreciate the profound works of voluminous historians; and if I had, I have no time to read them. But your series of Histories gives me, in brief compass, just that knowledge of past men and events which I need. I have read them with the greatest interest. To them I am indebted for about all the historical knowledge I have.*"

CYRUS THE GREAT.
DARIUS THE GREAT.
XERXES.
ALEXANDER THE GREAT.
ROMULUS.
HANNIBAL.
PYRRHUS.
JULIUS CÆSAR.
CLEOPATRA.
NERO.
ALFRED THE GREAT.
WILLIAM THE CONQUEROR.
RICHARD I.
RICHARD II.
RICHARD III.
MARY QUEEN OF SCOTS.
QUEEN ELIZABETH.
CHARLES I.
CHARLES II.
JOSEPHINE.
MARIA ANTOINETTE.
MADAME ROLAND.
HENRY IV.
PETER THE GREAT.
GENGHIS KHAN.
KING PHILIP.
HERNANDO CORTEZ.
MARGARET OF ANJOU.
JOSEPH BONAPARTE.
QUEEN HORTENSE.
LOUIS XIV.

MARCO PAUL SERIES.

Marco Paul's Voyages and Travels in the Pursuit of Knowledge. By JACOB ABBOTT. Beautifully Illustrated. Complete in 6 Volumes, 16mo, Cloth, 90 cents per Volume. Price of the set, in case, $5 40.

> **In New York.**
> **On the Erie Canal.**
> **In the Forests of Maine.**
> **In Vermont.**
> **In Boston.**
> **At the Springfield Armory.**

The design of these volumes is not simply to present a narrative of juvenile adventures, but also to communicate, in connection with them, a knowledge of the geography, scenery, and customs of the sections of country over which the young traveler is conducted. Marco Paul makes his journeyings under the guidance of a well-informed tutor, who takes care to give him all the information which he needs. The narrative is rendered still farther attractive by the introduction of personal incidents which would naturally befall the actors of the story. No American child can read this series without delight and instruction. But it will not be confined to the juvenile library. Presenting a vivid commentary on American society, manners, scenery, and institutions, it has a powerful charm for readers of all ages.

RAINBOW AND LUCKY SERIES.

By JACOB ABBOTT. Beautifully Illustrated. 16mo, Cloth, 90 cents each.

> **Handie,**
> **Rainbow's Journey.**
> **The Three Pines.**
> **Selling Lucky.**
> **Up the River.**

A new series of Juvenile Stories, by one of the most popular of American writers for young people. It abounds in the familiar details, lively descriptions, and happy illustrations, which give such an interest to Mr. Abbott's writings for young people.

THE LITTLE LEARNER SERIES.

A Series for Very Young Children. Designed to Assist in the Earliest Development of the Mind of a Child, while under its Mother's Special Care, during the first Five or Six Years of its Life. By Jacob Abbott. Beautifully Illustrated. Complete in 5 Small 4to Volumes, Cloth, 90 cents per Vol. Price of the set, in case, $4 50.

LEARNING TO TALK; or, Entertaining and Instructive Lessons in the Use of Language. 170 Engravings.

LEARNING TO THINK : consisting of Easy and Entertaining Lessons, designed to Assist in the First Unfolding of the Reflective and Reasoning Powers of Children. 120 Engravings.

LEARNING TO READ; consisting of Easy and Entertaining Lessons, designed to Assist Young Children in Studying the Forms of the Letters, and in beginning to Read. 160 Engravings.

LEARNING ABOUT COMMON THINGS; or, Familiar Instruction for Children in respect to the Objects around them that attract their Attention and awaken their Curiosity in the Earliest Years of Life. 120 Engravings.

LEARNING ABOUT RIGHT AND WRONG; or, Entertaining and Instructive Lessons for Young Children in respect to their Duty. 90 Engravings.

KINGS AND QUEENS.

KINGS AND QUEENS; or, Life in the Palace: consisting of Historical Sketches of Josephine and Maria Louisa, Louis Philippe, Ferdinand of Austria, Nicholas, Isabella II., Leopold, Victoria, and Louis Napoleon. By JOHN S. C. ABBOTT. With numerous Illustrations. 12mo, Cloth, $1 75.

It is extremely difficult to obtain accurate information respecting the character and conduct of those who occupy thrones. The views of writers are so influenced by political predilections, that the same character is represented by one as an angel, and by another as a demon. The author of these pages has spared no pains to obtain as correct knowledge as possible of the distinguished individuals of whom he has written, and he has introduced no illustrative actions which have not appeared to him to be well authenticated.

A SUMMER IN SCOTLAND.

A SUMMER IN SCOTLAND · a Narrative of Observations and Adventures made by the Author during a Summer spent among the Glens and Highlands in Scotland. By JOHN S. C. ABBOTT. Illustrated with Engravings. 12mo, Cloth, $1 75.

THE ROMANCE OF SPANISH HISTORY.

THE ROMANCE OF SPANISH HISTORY. By JOHN S. C. ABBOTT, Author of "The French Revolution," "The History of Napoleon Bonaparte," &c. With Illustrations. 12mo, Cloth, $2 00.

Miss Sedgwick's Works.

Miss Sedgwick has marked individuality; she writes with a higher aim than merely to amuse. Indeed, the rare endowments of her mind depend in an unusual degree upon the moral qualities with which they are united for their value. Animated by a cheerful philosophy, and anxious to pour its sunshine into every place where there is lurking care or suffering, she selects for illustration the scenes of every-day experience, paints them with exact fidelity, and seeks to diffuse over the mind a delicious serenity, and in the heart kind feelings and sympathies, and wise ambition, and steady hope. Her style is colloquial, picturesque, and marked by a facile grace, which is evidently a gift of nature. Her characters are nicely drawn and delicately contrasted; her delineation of manners decidedly the best that have appeared.—*Prose Writers of America.*

MEMOIR OF JOSEPH CURTIS. A Model Man. By the Author of "Married or Single?" "Means and Ends," "The Linwoods," "Hope Leslie," "Live and Let Live," &c., &c. 16mo, Muslin, 75 cents.

MARRIED OR SINGLE? By Miss CATHARINE M. SEDGWICK, Author of "Hope Leslie," "The Linwoods," "Means and Ends," "Live and Let Live," &c., &c. 2 vols. 12mo, Muslin, $3 co.

LIVE AND LET LIVE; or, Domestic Service Illustrated. By Miss C. M. SEDGWICK. 18mo, Muslin, 75 cents.

MEANS AND ENDS; or, Self-training. By Miss C. M. SEDGWICK. 18mo, Muslin, 75 cents.

A LOVE TOKEN FOR CHILDREN. Designed for Sunday-School Libraries. By Miss C. M. SEDGWICK. 18mo, Muslin, 75 cents.

THE POOR RICH MAN AND THE RICH POOR MAN. By Miss C. M. SEDGWICK. 18mo, Muslin, 75 cents.

STORIES FOR YOUNG PERSONS. By Miss C. M. SEDGWICK. 18mo, Muslin, 75 cents.

WILTON HARVEY, AND OTHER TALES. By Miss C. M. SEDGWICK. 18mo, Muslin, 75 cents.

www.ingramcontent.com/pod-product-compliance
Lightning Source LLC
Chambersburg PA
CBHW030323270326
41926CB00010B/1475